Overcoming Paralyzing Doubt & Indecision

A CBT Workbook to Conquer the Fear, Uncertainty & Anxiety That Keep You Stuck

DAVID A. CLARK, PhD

New Harbinger Publications, Inc.

Publisher's Note

NEW HARBINGER PUBLICATIONS is a registered trademark of New Harbinger Publications, Inc.

New Harbinger Publications is an employee-owned company.

Copyright © 2026 by David A. Clark
New Harbinger Publications, Inc.
5720 Shattuck Avenue
Oakland, CA 94609
www.newharbinger.com

Cover design by Amy Shoup

Acquired by Ryan Buresh

Edited by James Lainsbury

Library of Congress Cataloging-in-Publication Data on file

Printed in the United States of America

28   27   26

10   9   8   7   6   5   4   3   2   1   First Printing

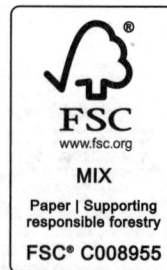

"David A. Clark offers a compassionate and practical road map for breaking free from chronic doubt. Readers will feel understood, empowered, and ready to move forward."

—**Jonathan S. Abramowitz, PhD**, professor of clinical psychology at the University of North Carolina at Chapel Hill, and author of *Getting Over OCD*

"In accessible language, David A. Clark demonstrates how to make decisions and take actions when doubt is present. Seeking safety or certainty will usually backfire. There are relevant distinctions between opinion, belief, and conviction; between self-doubt and low risk tolerance; and between healthy and unhealthy doubt in relationships. Self-tests and personalized exercises assist the reader to identify specific thinking mistakes and beliefs to illuminate the path forward. I highly recommend this book."

—**Sally Winston, PsyD**, coauthor of *Overcoming Unwanted Intrusive Thoughts*, *Needing to Know for Sure*, and *Overcoming Anticipatory Anxiety*

"Written by one of the world's leading experts in cognitive behavioral therapy (CBT), this helpful workbook thoughtfully describes doubt and indecisiveness, and how to put science-driven tools to work to overcome what can often be incredibly debilitating—the struggle with not being sure. The book contains examples, worksheets, tips, and strategies, and is likely to be most useful to those seeking relief from their own doubts across a range of domains."

—**Adam S. Radomsky, PhD**, professor of psychology at Concordia University, director of the Anxiety and OCD Laboratory, and founding president of the Canadian Association of Cognitive and Behavioural Therapies

"In this world, nothing is certain but death, taxes, and that this book is an antidote to doubt. Crisp, clear analysis of the doubting cycle and how to break out of it from an esteemed authority who has dedicated his career to helping people overcome stuck thinking patterns. Full of useful hints and creative strategies to redirect your mind from doubt to freedom."

—**Christine Purdon, PhD, CPsych**, professor of psychology at the University of Waterloo

"Uncertainty is the essence of life. Our past, our present, and the future we can't yet see are wrapped in distressful doubts. It's fine for most of us, but not for all, not always. This workbook, the result of David A. Clark's considerable clinical and research work, offers clear intervention strategies and compassionate guidance—and helps us make friends with uncertainty and debilitating, unhealthy, unhelpful, uncontrollable, and mind-polluting doubts and indecisiveness."

> —**Gregoris Simos, MD, PhD**, professor of psychopathology at the University of Macedonia, and member of the Beck Institute International Advisory Committee

"This fantastic resource offers accessible tools to identify and understand paralyzing doubt, indecision, uncertainty, and perfectionism; to shift away from the strategies that keep you stuck; and to implement flexible, evidence-based approaches to deal more effectively with doubt and its associated challenges."

> —**Jed Siev, PhD**, associate professor of psychology at Swarthmore College

"David has written an astoundingly clear book that places perfectionism and the quest for certainty at the heart of doubt. Doubt is a neglected construct in the literature, yet it is everywhere in daily life. Finally, we have a road map that helps us navigate and manage the traps that maintain doubt."

> —**Sunil Bhar, PhD**, professor of psychology at Swinburne University, and coeditor of *The Self in Understanding and Treating Psychological Disorders*

Contents

Foreword

Anyone who is reflective and has a critical mind will find that they doubt something at some time. I know that I have had doubts about religion, politics, the media, academics, friends and colleagues, and even my values at times. If Descartes thought that the only thing he could not doubt was that he exists—"I think, therefore I am"—I would update this to say, "I doubt, therefore I am human." The ability of humans to think of the possible, not just the actual, adds to our unique capacity for doubt, regret, and worry. There are certain things that come with the territory and doubt is one of them.

In fact, doubt can be the beginning of innovation, progress, or finding an alternative perspective and course of action. It's part of being human. One could argue that progress begins with doubt. The Enlightenment doubted the authority of conventional religion and tradition. Technical breakthroughs in all areas begin with doubting the validity of what has been done for many years. But doubt can also be a process that stops you from making decisions, that keeps you worried and ruminating, and that challenges your very sense of identity. This is the focus of David A. Clark's excellent book, Overcoming Paralyzing Doubt and Indecision.

We are all confronted with uncertainty, every day of our lives. But the problematic doubter treats uncertainty as something that is intolerable and a sign that something bad not only could go wrong, but is likely to go wrong. You might google the maladies that you fear for hours without ever reaching certainty, and then this adds to your doubt. Clark gives examples from his clinical experience of how the intolerance of uncertainty, the pursuit of conviction, the demand for a perfect solution, and the fear of any reasonable risk can keep you frozen in your tracks. As you turn to others for reassurance, collect more information, wait to feel ready, the opportunities of a full life pass you by. The world is not going to wait for you to reconcile your doubts and find certainty. It goes on. Without you.

We can all come up with questions that add to our doubt, but then we need to ask ourselves, "How can I live in the real world?" There is no certainty in an uncertain world. Decisions are not about no risk—they are about one risk versus another risk. And reassurance seeking will inevitably lead to you questioning the credentials of the person giving the reassurance. Life is not without downsides or even disasters. It's about trade-offs. Are you willing to accept some uncertainty and the possibility of a bad outcome to dig yourself out of the ever-deepening hole of your perennial doubts? You could continue asking questions. But if there is no answer that will suffice, you have tethered yourself to a constant interrogation with no end.

Living your life is not the same thing as the absence of doubt. Living your life is about—well, living. No one says, at the end of their life, "I'm really glad I doubted everything and sought certainty." What they say is: "I wish that I had been true to my feelings, that I had connected with the people I love, and that I had done what I really wanted to do, not what others wanted me to do."

Living life is about action, connection, taking chances, experiencing the full range of emotions, and accepting the noise of your doubts as the occasional storm that you walk through. You have to go through it to get past it. Standing on the threshold with your doubts will not get you into your life.

This book is what publishers call "a smart book"—that is, it doesn't just give you the tools to use to make progress; it helps you understand why you are stuck in the same philosophical merry-go-round of questioning and rejecting answers. Dr. Clark is an unusual academic researcher. He actually sees patients, and he integrates his real-world experiences with his vast knowledge of cognitive behavioral therapy. It is the perfect combination for a self-help book author.

This is a book that can help you live the life that you want to live. Not without doubts, but by putting your doubts in perspective, making room for tradeoffs and downsides and uncertainty, and replacing the perfect with the real and obtainable. If you want to live your life, take the leap of faith across the threshold, and walk through the door.

—Robert Leahy, PhD
Author of Don't Believe Everything You Feel

The Absurdity of Doubt

Do you often get an unsettled feeling that something you did or a decision you made is not quite right? It's a nagging feeling, a question that just won't go away. *Should I have made that purchase? Did I leave enough tip at the restaurant? Should I take this job offer? Is this relationship right for me?* One common thread runs through these questions: doubt.

Are you a doubter? Is it hard to let go of past actions or decisions? Have you ever been paralyzed with indecision—so much so you couldn't respond to a situation you found yourself in? For some of us, doubt is a persistent and unrelenting torment that is a root cause of anxiety, worry, irritability, and guilt. When doubt is overwhelming, it can sabotage decision making, undermine personal effectiveness, and cause considerable anguish and despair.

> Persistent, uncontrollable doubt causes significant emotional distress and damages personal effectiveness, resilience, and resourcefulness.

We can't live without doubt. It's a normal, necessary process of the human brain. No one teaches us how to doubt; we all do it quite naturally without effort or training. Because we can imagine possibilities, what might happen in the future or could have been different in the past, we are able to doubt. Our capacity for creativity is fertile soil for doubt. But doubt can be difficult to control and so is often an unwanted, annoying mental intrusion.

Although doubt is an experience known to all, it remains a mystery to most. You know what it's like to doubt, but do you know what it is? And that's what makes doubt so absurd. We know how it feels, but it's hard to explain. If you "doubt" this statement, how would you explain doubt to a nonhuman alien?

Doubt is…

Doubt varies in intensity and duration, and the focus of our doubts is intricately connected to what is most significant to us: past decisions, current concerns, and aspirations for the future. For some, doubt is a faint voice, an occasional intrusion of the mind that whispers *Are you sure?* and causes you to stop and reconsider before taking some action or making a decision. But for others, doubt is an unrelenting, nagging state of intolerable uncertainty that causes indecision, mental anguish, and paralysis in action. Doubt that is excessive can cause mental health problems and destroy cherished goals and ambitions. When this happens, the problem of doubt cannot be ignored.

It is possible to doubt anything and everything, from our most routine, mundane actions to significant life-changing decisions. Who hasn't doubted whether they locked the door, turned off the stove, or showed enough appreciation for a kind favor? And then there are the most important life decisions. *Should I make a lifelong commitment to this person? Should I take this job offer or stay put? Should we have children?* We can have doubts about the future, or we can doubt our past actions and decisions. The former can lead to worry, the latter to rumination and regret.

This is a workbook about doubt, in all its various forms and intensities. It drills into the experience of doubt and explains why it is often at the root of many mental health problems, such as obsessive-compulsive disorder (OCD), anxiety, worry, and depression. You'll learn that doubt is the cause of many personal problems, such as fear of commitment and low self-esteem, and even crises of faith for the religiously devout. But doubt is not always harmful. There is a healthy form of doubt that can boost personal effectiveness, promote independence, and improve quality of life. If you struggle with excessive doubt, this book will help you gain a better understanding of what it actually is, and I'll show you how to transform the doubt that currently holds you back into more productive ways of thinking. But first, let's take a closer look at this mental process called "doubt."

What Is Doubt?

Doubt is a mental state that involves a feeling of uncertainty in which judgment is suspended concerning the correctness of certain facts, beliefs, actions, motives, or decisions. Doubt is a way of thinking, what psychologists call a *cognitive process* (O'Connor et al. 2005), which means that just about any experience, whether past, present, or anticipated, can be doubted. To better understand this process, let's look at three common categories of doubt.

> Doubt is the repeated questioning of possibilities due to a feeling of uncertainty about the best action or decision and often results in a suspended judgment or decision.

Doubt About Past Actions

Do your doubts often start with *Did I…* or *Should I have…?* If so, it's likely you're thinking about some past action, comment, or decision. *Did I show enough appreciation for that gift? Should I have purchased that new piece of furniture? Did I make the right choice in taking this new job?* Almost any past action or decision can elicit a sense of doubt. So why is it that some people can be so confident in their actions and decisions, whereas others get stuck in doubt, second-guessing what they did in the past?

The first reason that people get stuck in doubt is their concern that an action, comment, or decision didn't allow them to avoid some possible harm, wasn't done correctly or completely, or failed to result in a desired level of satisfaction (Chiang and Purdon 2023). For example, you're racked with doubts—that is, uncertainty—over whether your comments hurt your sister-in-law's feelings. Thinking you may have offended her and now there could be significant family conflict fuels your doubt. You care a great deal about your family relationships, so the possibility that you've caused trouble is important to you. Clearly this doubt is worthy of your attention.

Doubts about the past also develop from a lack of conviction or a lack of a "feeling of knowing" that what you did, thought, or felt is accurate or correct (Lazarov et al. 2012). This happens when you don't trust your sensory information (what you saw, heard, touched, and so forth), or you require more information before you can be convinced something is okay, that you can leave the past alone. *Buyer's remorse* is a good example of this dilemma. For example, let's say you made a big purchase but now have doubts because you don't trust what you were told at the time of purchase. You feel like you need more information to confirm that you made the right decision.

A low confidence in one's memory is another major source of doubts about the past. You're trying hard to remember what you said to your sister-in-law but feel like there are gaps in your memory. You're unsure of your recollection of the conversation, which fuels doubt.

Do you often have persistent doubts about past actions, comments, or decisions? Does the doubting feel uncontrollable, leaving you frustrated, annoyed, or anxious? Take a few minutes to consider whether you have doubts about your actions and decisions.

> Persistent doubt about past actions or decisions is a core feature of obsessive thinking.

EXERCISE: Doubts About Past Actions and Decisions

Think about all the activities, conversations, decisions, and other responsibilities you faced this past month. Did persistent doubt play a role in any of these experiences? List two to three past experiences for which you remember questioning yourself, critically evaluating whether you'd made the right decision or taken the correct course of action.

1. _____

2. _____

3. _____

What do you notice from the experiences you listed? Was the doubt intense, persistent, and uncontrollable? Maybe you told yourself to *forget about it*, whatever *it* was, but you couldn't let it go; you were stuck in doubt. Or was the doubt more a momentary mental intrusion that you were able to move past? If the doubting experiences you listed feel persistent, uncontrollable, and distressing, you'll want to return to this list after I've introduced you to strategies for dealing with problematic doubt in part 3 of the book.

Doubt and Indecision

Decision making involves selecting an option from several alternatives that are associated with a different outcome (Lee 2013). Life is full of decision-making opportunities. We can't go a single day without encountering them. There are the small, continuous decisions necessary to living day to day: what to wear, what to eat, when to speak up or be silent, where to go, and what to do. And then there are the life-changing decisions that center on family, work, health, finances, relationships, and the like.

How would you characterize your decision-making ability? Do you find decision making stressful? Are you often paralyzed by indecision and so miss out on good opportunities because you can't decide what to do? If you find yourself in an enduring state of indecision, your anxiety will rise and you will be annoyed with yourself for hesitating. When debilitating indecision sets in, excessive doubt is the culprit causing your mental torment.

> Excessive doubt impairs decision making and can lead to a sense of paralysis, stagnation, and defeatism.

There are two elements of indecision that can turn it into a chronic state. The first is intolerance of uncertainty. When making a decision, you're faced with different options that will have consequences you cannot fully know. There are risks associated with any decision because the future cannot be known with any degree of certainty; it can only be predicted. If your tolerance for uncertainty is low, you may delay choosing an option because you fear an unfavorable outcome.

Let's say you're house hunting. You've looked at several desirable properties, but you can't make up your mind. There are pros and cons for each property, and so you're in a state of indecision. When you start to make a decision, doubts arise, and so you hesitate. You lose out on several possibilities because of your indecision. There will always be uncertainty when one takes the plunge and makes an offer on a house. Will you be able to get a good price for your existing property? Is your bid too high or too low? Will the new house require costly upgrades? If you're risk aversive and can't stand uncertainty, you'll be indecisive.

A focus on minimizing the potential costs associated with different options, the second element associated with chronic indecision, tends to delay decision making. In the house-hunting example, if you're more concerned with reducing the negative consequences of your decision than about the advantages of your choice, you'll be more indecisive. Also, there's a tendency to interpret the presence of doubt as meaningful and significant (Chiang and Purdon 2023). This will also contribute to your state of indecision. For example, as you look at one house after another, you will see something wrong with each property. This will increase your doubt about the desirability of that property, so you will delay your decision. But then the house sells, and you will have missed another opportunity.

Are you an indecisive person? Do you feel stressed and anxious even with the minor, routine decisions of daily living? Or are you facing some major decisions in your life that are driving your indecision to paralyzing levels? Take a moment to consider the major and minor decisions you are currently facing.

EXERCISE: Experiences of Indecision

In the space below write down any challenging decision-making opportunities you are facing. Focus on examples that make you feel anxious, stressed, and indecisive.

1. _____

2. _____

3. _____

Are experiences of indecision causing you considerable personal distress? Can you see how excessive doubt plays a role in your indecision? As we consider the problem of chronic indecision in subsequent chapters, you'll want to refer back to the experiences you listed in this exercise.

Doubt About Core Beliefs

A *belief* is a mental representation of phenomena in the physical world or of something abstract that we are convinced is true. It is an assumption that we think is true because of our own experience, or because of what we are taught by others, such as our family, friends, media, and social institutions. Our beliefs inform us about the world, especially how to function in a highly interpersonal environment. So, what we believe influences our behavior, thoughts, feelings, and relations with others. Some beliefs are highly specific and less central to defining who we are. *I should be courteous and hold the door open for others, I should not be rude and interrupt a person who is talking,* or *It's important to save a little from my monthly salary* are examples of beliefs that guide our behavior in specific situations.

Core beliefs are beliefs that are central to how we understand our self, the world, and other people. There are negative core beliefs, like *I am worthless, Other people can't be trusted,* and *The world is an unsafe place,* and there are positive core beliefs, like *I'm quite resourceful and can rely on myself, Most people are good and kind,* and *Everyone should be treated equally.* Generally, we are more invested in our core beliefs and so tend to have strong conviction in their truthfulness.

> A feeling of uncertainty about your worth or value, moral standards, or matters of faith is a form of existential doubt that is especially unsettling because it challenges your core beliefs.

Doubt can play havoc with our beliefs, especially core beliefs. It can be quite distressing to be confronted with an experience or information that is contrary to or incongruent with a core belief. The inconsistency may cause you to question the accuracy and truthfulness of the belief, or you may completely distort or discount the incongruent information to resolve the inconsistency with your belief. Let's say one of your core beliefs is *I'm a friendly person who is liked, valued, and respected by others.* But then you experience a series of rejections by people you thought were your friends. As a result you begin to doubt the core belief that you're valued and respected by others. In turn this doubt may cause a crisis in your self-identity, a flood of negative emotions, and your withdrawal from others.

It's particularly important to consider how doubt affects beliefs about self-identity, beliefs about religious faith, and beliefs about morality. Doubts in these domains have the greatest impact on our emotional health and well-being. For example, people with an elevated level of religious doubt have more symptoms of anxiety and depression and a lower sense of well-being (Upenieks 2021). Doubts about moral beliefs—standards we hold about how others are treated that focus on concerns like harm, care, fairness, loyalty, respect of authority, and decency (Graham et al. 2011)—can negatively impact our interpersonal relationships by eroding our trust in others and curtailing our care, compassion, and empathy for others. Cognitive behavioral therapy (CBT) for anxiety and depression has long recognized the importance of building up positive, adaptive core beliefs about the self to overcome symptoms of emotional distress.

Do you have questions and uncertainties about your self-worth and value, long-held moral standards and convictions, or religious teachings and beliefs? The next exercise provides an opportunity to list such doubts.

EXERCISE: Doubts About Core Beliefs

To determine whether you have significant doubts about core beliefs, think about experiences that caused you to question your strengths and abilities (self-worth), to reevaluate certain moral judgments, or to question basic religious beliefs. List the specific doubts you have felt because of these experiences.

1. _____

2. _____

3. _____

4. _____

5. _____

If you're not sure whether you have doubts about core beliefs, consider the following example. After graduating from college with a degree in business, Morgan took a job as a junior financial advisor at a large bank. Transitioning from the safety and security of her family into a new, independent life raised serious doubts about several of her core beliefs.

1. When I compare myself to coworkers, I wonder if I'm not as smart and competent as I thought.

2. Maybe I can't be completely honest with people.

3. Can people really be trusted? Maybe trust has to be earned.

4. I was raised to believe that God is directing my life, but I have my doubts. Maybe things just happen by chance.

Like Morgan, have you had experiences that challenged some of your core beliefs? Have your religious or spiritual beliefs been shaken by doubt? Do you often experience *imposter syndrome,* in which you feel like a fraud whose incompetence will soon be discovered by others? If these questions resonate with you, you'll want to work on core belief doubts in subsequent chapters.

Extreme Doubt

How bad can it get? Is it possible for doubt to be so toxic that it threatens the very fabric of our thought processes? This is exactly what happens when you begin to question your identity and very existence. When you find yourself in this place, doubt has infiltrated such fundamental thought processes that meeting the demands of everyday living is threatened. This form of existential doubt occurs when you question the accuracy of your five senses (taste, smell, vision, hearing, and touch). *Does my experience reflect true reality, or is it possible I'm living an alternate reality?* When you start questioning reality, your very existence, doubt can be so distressing that it is almost unbearable.

Emma struggled with existential doubt after watching several fantasy movies, including *The Matrix*, *The Butterfly Effect*, and *Possible Worlds*. Although drawn to this film genre, she felt deeply troubled by the plots of these movies. For weeks afterward she found herself reanalyzing their plausibility, which caused her to think deeply about her own reality. *How do we know that what we experience is real? Am I living in an alternate reality, with real existence beyond my own experience? How can I trust what I see, hear, and feel?* Emma had nightmares of getting caught in a parallel universe, alone and cut off from the rest of humanity. During the day, her mind was preoccupied with existential doubt. The mental anguish caused by the doubt was unrelenting and uncontrollable. She found it increasingly hard to focus on her work or family responsibilities. She decided that pursuing knowledge was the best answer to her mental turmoil. She searched online for information about how the brain functions and whether our perceptions reflect a "true" reality or are mere constructions of an imaginative brain, but none of the answers she found satisfactorily addressed her doubts.

This unrelenting doubt about her existence had a profound effect on Emma's mental health. Anxiety became the emotion that dominated her day. She developed certain compulsive rituals, such as repeated checking and endless reanalyzing, that seemed to magically ease anxiety some of the time. Emma became more isolated and reclusive in an attempt to avoid anything that would trigger her existential doubts. And she spent hours and hours reading works on philosophy, religion, neuroscience, psychology, and psychiatry to find convincing proof that she was experiencing true reality. But these efforts proved futile. Emma was spiraling down a wormhole of doubt that was wrecking her life.

> In its most extreme form, doubt can make even the most basic functions like what to say or how to act an agonizing process that causes serious mental distress.

Emma's doubt about reality and whether she might be living in an alternate universe is an example of extreme doubt. After all, what could be more fundamental to living than questioning the very essence of life itself? Most likely you have more certainty about reality than Emma, but you might have doubts about other aspects of your identity that are challenging core beliefs about who you are and your place in this world.

Healthy Doubt

If doubt can be so disruptive that you question even your own existence, you might be thinking that doubt serves no good purpose. But in reality a little doubt can go a long way in enriching our life, making us more resourceful, resilient, and self-reliant.

For most people a meaningful life is characterized by striving to reach goals and aspirations for our relationships, work, health, community, and spirituality. Psychologists have long recognized that certain cognitive skills, or one's thinking ability, are essential to thriving in this life. Various terms are used to describe these skills, including critical thinking, higher-order thinking, problem solving, and decision making. Identifying and clarifying a problem or issue, objectively evaluating the feasibility of several alternatives, and then testing out the different alternatives to determine the best solution are common processes of this type of thinking. Doubt is an indispensable process in critical thinking. It's the process that causes you to question every idea or piece of information regarding an issue at hand. A critical thinker doesn't automatically accept everything they are told. Instead, doubt helps them suspend judgment on the truthfulness of information until further evidence is gathered.

Take Elena, who faced a critical decision in her life. She poured everything into developing an accounting career and rose to the position of senior partner in a large firm. Now in her early sixties, she can go no further in her career and wonders if it's time to retire. She's been with the same firm for thirty-seven years and is feeling burned-out. She could take early retirement and start living off her pension and savings, or she could continue to work until turning seventy, an option several colleagues have chosen. It is an agonizing decision, because if she chooses early retirement, there is no turning back.

> Critical thinking, problem solving, and reasoning would not be possible without the presence of doubt that causes a suspension in judgment until further information is obtained.

As with so many decisions in her life, Elena used doubt to sharpen her critical thinking skills to arrive at a satisfactory decision. She started by clarifying what was making this decision so anxiety provoking. She realized she was afraid that if she stayed until she was seventy, her clients and work colleagues might start questioning her competence. Like many workers nearing the end of their careers, she worried that she might begin losing her edge and start making mistakes, and this could damage her stellar reputation. On the other hand, she might become bored and depressed in retirement, having lost a key source of purpose in life.

The next step in her decision-making process was to gather as much evidence as possible on the costs and benefits of staying versus taking early retirement. This is where doubt was most helpful. Rather than accept each cost or benefit at face value, doubt helped Elena suspend judgment and evaluate each point objectively. She used considerable research and reflection to determine the true merits of each cost and benefit. She also did not assign any inherent significance to the presence of doubt, rather she used its presence as a signal to pause her thinking and ask, *Have I given due diligence to this point?*

Finally, Elena realized that whatever she decided based on her cost-benefit analysis, she could never completely eliminate doubt. She recognized that every decision involves risk and uncertainty because the future can only be predicted, not known. She did not interpret doubt's presence as an indicator of a wrong decision, but rather she saw it as an inevitability of decision making. In this way doubt remained a healthy coping strategy rather than a disruptive mental intrusion.

Like Elena, have you faced important life decisions in recent years? Has doubt been an asset or a liability in your decision making? Use the following exercise to consider whether you've been able to harness the power of doubt.

EXERCISE: The Positive Doubt Checklist

Think back to some of your major decisions. Use the checklist below to assess the extent to which doubt facilitated your decision making in a positive manner. Place a checkmark beside each statement that describes your experience of doubt.

- ☐ Doubt motivated me to reexamine information relevant to the decision.

- ☐ Doubt sharpened my focus on critical aspects of the decision.

- ☐ I considered doubt a natural part of the decision-making process.

- ☐ I did not become distracted or upset by the presence of doubt.

- ☐ I was able to be more rational, objective, and realistic in my decision making because doubt prevented me from jumping to conclusions.

If you checked three or more statements, it is likely that you have positive experiences of doubt. On the other hand, maybe you rarely experience doubt as it's reflected in these statements, and doubt is more a hindrance than a help in your decision making. If this is so, take heart; learning how to harness your doubt to boost your decision-making powers is the focus of this workbook.

What to Expect

Has this chapter opened your eyes to the complexity of doubt? Maybe you've long known your tendency to doubt has gotten in the way and made your life harder. Or maybe you've never given doubt much thought, but now you're wondering if excessive doubt might be a root cause of your anxiety, guilt, or other emotional distress. If you're left with more questions than answers about doubt, I encourage you to read on. This is a workbook for doubters. You'll learn how to better understand your experience of doubt, and you'll be introduced to strategies for turning negative doubt into a more positive, helpful mental strategy. Here's what you can expect in the remaining chapters.

Chapters 1 through 5 pull back the curtain on the mysteries of doubt. You'll learn about the five key processes that characterize doubt: the pursuit of certainty, indecision, the need for conviction, perfectionism, and aversion to taking risks. A deeper understanding of these core processes is integral to learning how to identify excessive doubt and transform it into a healthy search for answers.

Part 2 delves into the many ways that doubt affects our life. Chapters 6 through 8 consider obsessive doubt, relationship doubt, and moral/faith-based doubt. The last three chapters, part 3, present intervention strategies for doubt. You'll want to spend extra time with these chapters, in which you'll find step-by-step instructions, exercises, and worksheets to help you transform your experience of doubt. Many of these worksheets are available for download from the website for this book, http://www.newharbinger.com/55756.

Maybe you've struggled with doubt for years. Or perhaps you've never considered whether doubt may be fueling your anxiety, depression, or obsessive tendencies. Or maybe you've been hampered by indecision, fear of commitment, or lack of confidence. This workbook is designed to increase your understanding of doubt and help you sharpen your skills for using it in a positive and adaptive way. So, whatever your experience of doubt, I invite you to begin your own journey, using this workbook as your guide.

PART 1

Dismantling Doubt

CHAPTER 1

The Problem of Uncertainty

No doubt you've heard the expression "In this world nothing is certain but death and taxes," a comment attributed to Benjamin Franklin. Although the juxtaposition of taxes with death is meant to be humorous, the first part of the statement is probably the most truthful. *Nothing in this world is certain!* Of course, death is certain for all, but we have complete certainty of life only at the moment something happens. We have expectations about the future, we make plans and predict what might happen in the next hours, days, or even years, but life throws us curveballs. The future can be anticipated but remains unknown until it's experienced. We long to know what lies ahead, so we look for signs, evidence of what will happen—anything that can strengthen our predictions, so we're better prepared for the future. We are attempting to bring some degree of certainty to an uncertain world, and therein lies the seeds of doubt.

Being certain is more important to some than to others. Are you a person who can go with the flow of life, or do you like to know what lies ahead so you can plan and prepare for the best or the worst to come? If you have a strong need to know (see chapter 3), then you probably desire a greater degree of certainty. And when you can't achieve certainty, you doubt. The less certain you are, the more persistent and intense the doubt.

This is a chapter about uncertainty. Uncertainty is the core process in doubt. It's the presence of uncertainty that causes doubt. It would be impossible to have doubt about a decision you're certain was best under the circumstances. Ultimately, your relationship with

> Uncertainty is an indelible aspect of life. We cannot escape uncertainty or eliminate it from our daily experience.

uncertainty will determine your experience of doubt. If you are quite tolerant of uncertainty, doubt will be minimal. But if you find uncertainty distressing and intolerable, doubt will rear its ugly head and cause considerable emotional distress.

To understand doubt, you must first understand uncertainty and why some people struggle so hard when facing it. So, we'll start with a definition of uncertainty and its relation to doubt. Then I'll identify the key elements of uncertainty and provide tools you can use to determine how well you accept uncertainty. By the end of this chapter, you'll have learned whether a pursuit of greater (or even perfect) certainty is causing you to doubt. Before we begin, consider Tiffany's struggle with doubt that was rooted in her intolerance of uncertainty.

Tiffany's Story: *An Overwhelming Sense of Uncertainty*

By her own admission Tiffany was a chronic doubter. If asked a question about anything, she couldn't give a straight answer, qualifying everything with "I think...," "I'm not sure but it could be...," or "Maybe..." Procrastination and indecision were huge problems for her. She always tried to get others to decide for her. To others she came across as skeptical and mistrustful because she questioned everything she heard. Tiffany's doubt caused her to worry incessantly about the future and ruminate about past actions and decisions. Needless to say, she was often anxious and worried to the point of considerable personal distress, and these emotions interfered with her ability to work and take care of her family. Let's look at examples of how doubt interfered with Tiffany's life.

Tiffany purchased a new refrigerator and ended up paying more than she expected to. Immediately she experienced a severe case of buyer's remorse; she was overcome with doubts about whether she had made the right decision. *Did I pay too much? Did I buy the right brand, one that will last for years? Have I been extravagant with my purchase? Can we really afford it? Maybe the old fridge would have lasted a few more years?* Uncertainty was at the root of all these questions that were causing Tiffany to doubt the correctness of her purchase.

A more serious decision involved her ten-year-old son's poor school performance. Extensive testing revealed a learning disability, but little progress had been made with remedial help. So Tiffany explored the possibility of sending him to a private school that specialized in helping students with learning problems. But the tuition was expensive and would put a terrible strain on the family's finances. Tiffany did lots of research, talked to teachers and other experts, but remained undecided. She was paralyzed by doubt. *Can this school really improve my son's learning? How will he adapt to a new school? Will he feel stigmatized? Will he be able to make new friends? How can we afford it?* The uncertainty was almost impossible to address because of the potential long-term consequences of her decision. So, Tiffany was left with agonizing doubt over whether to send her son to the private school or keep him in his current public school.

Whether facing a minor decision of daily living or more important, life-changing issues, Tiffany experienced excessive doubt, all driven by an inability to deal with uncertainty. If all Tiffany's questions could be answered, there would be sublime certainty and no doubt. But in most cases the questions had no clear answers, and so she was left in a state of crippling uncertainty.

Uncertainty and Doubt

In many respects uncertainty and doubt are so intertwined that we can consider them two sides of a coin. *Uncertainty* is to experience an unknown about a result or an outcome (Carleton 2016). It's a simple word with a more complicated meaning. You can have either a positive or negative experience when confronted with uncertainty. Let's say you're planning a trip. There are many unknowns when traveling to a new destination. You might find these uncertainties distressing if you are a planner and don't like surprises. On the other hand, you might find the unknown exhilarating and see it as an opportunity to explore and learn new things. How you experience uncertainty depends on how you respond to the unknown.

> *Uncertainty* is our experience of the unknown at any moment in time. If the experience is distressing, we're motivated to reduce uncertainty by pursuing a greater sense of knowing.

As defined in the book's introduction, *doubt* is the repeated questioning of possibilities due to a feeling of uncertainty. Uncertainty is the central experience of doubt. It's hard to imagine doubt will arise when you're certain of a result or outcome. For example, when the alarm goes off on a Tuesday morning, Tiffany is certain of her morning routine: Get ready for work, get my son to school, and drive to work. There is no indecision or doubt. She gets up and does what has to be done. But if on the way to work traffic is unusually heavy, doubt creeps in. *Will I be late for work? Should I take an alternate, longer route that has less traffic?* Such a decision is fraught with uncertainties because she can't know which choice will get her to work on time, so Tiffany doubts. And she can feel her anxiety and worry increase as she frets over what to do.

The following figure illustrates the relationship between uncertainty and doubt. As you can see, doubt always involves uncertainty, but you can experience uncertainty without doubt.

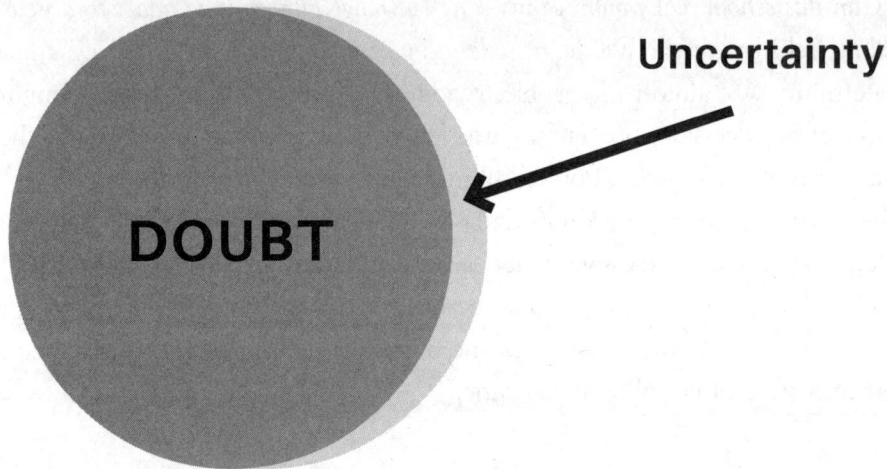

For example, if you hear a weather forecast that says there is an 80 percent chance of rain, you can't say for certain that it will rain—there is still some uncertainty in this percentage—but you have no doubts, experience no indecision, when deciding to take an umbrella. There is a very good chance it will rain.

This discussion about doubt and uncertainty is important because we'll be spending a lot of time focused on uncertainty and your ability to deal with the unknown. Tolerance of uncertainty is key to overcoming excessive doubt. At the same time, there's more to doubt than uncertainty, so it's important to treat them as distinct from each other. Use the next exercise to consider your experience of uncertainty and doubt.

EXERCISE: Connecting Doubt and Uncertainty

Recall some experiences of doubt and list them in the first column. In the second column write down any relevant information about the situation. These will be your "knowns." In the third column list what you didn't know about the situation. These "unknowns" are most important in driving your uncertainty and doubt. Tiffany's example appears in the first row.

Situation I Doubted	What I Knew	What I Didn't Know
My car is twelve years old and needs costly repairs. Should I put money into the car or trade it in for a newer but more expensive model?	• My car is old and will not last more than three to five years even with repairs. • Paying for repairs is cheaper than car payments. • I can't afford car payments and my son's private school. • I need a car to get to work.	• I don't know how many more years I can get out of the car. • I might repair it and then have another major repair bill soon after. • It's an old car and so it's unreliable; it's likely to break down when I least expect it.

Situation I Doubted	What I Knew	What I Didn't Know

No wonder Tiffany was experiencing considerable doubt and uncertainty about her car. She had as many unknowns as knowns, and it was the unknowns that increased her uncertainty about the best decision. What is the ratio of unknowns to knowns in the doubt experiences you listed? Some unknowns may be more important than the knowns, so it's not simply a matter of counting the two columns. The level of your uncertainty will depend on the number *and* significance of the unknowns. If you had difficulty recalling doubt experiences, keep track of such experiences over the next two to three weeks and record them on this worksheet, which you can download, along with other worksheets for this book, at http://www.newharbinger.com/55756.

Intolerance of Uncertainty

It's easy to recognize differences in people's ability to tolerate pain. Some people quickly turn to a pain reliever if they have a tension headache, whereas others will tough it out, hoping it'll go away on its own. We would say the first person has low tolerance for pain and the other person high tolerance. Tolerance for uncertainty is a lot like tolerance for pain in that people's ability to tolerate uncertainty differs greatly. The lower your tolerance for uncertainty, the greater the likelihood you'll experience doubt, anxiety, and worry when confronting the unknown of a situation.

Intolerance of uncertainty (IU) refers to a person's inability to endure the distress produced by a perceived absence of sufficient information to deal with a situation when the outcome is unknown (Carleton 2016; Freeston et al. 2020). People with the IU personality trait experience uncertain situations as distressing and difficult to manage, so they avoid them (Robichaud and Buhr 2018). For example, if your child complains of a stomachache as you're getting her ready for school, do you send her to school or keep her home? It's hard to know what to do. There are a lot of unknowns and uncertainties involved with making this decision. A person with high IU would find this situation very distressing and be tormented with doubt. A low-IU person would feel calmer about the situation and work out a contingency plan with greater confidence and flexibility.

> People with high intolerance of uncertainty experience more doubt and distress when confronted with the unknowns of a situation. They will try to avoid uncertainty or at least minimize it even to their own detriment.

Are you wondering if you have high IU? You can find out by completing the next exercise. It'll help you decide whether your IU is low (you can tolerate considerable uncertainty), moderate (in the middle range), or high (uncertainty is distressing, intolerable).

EXERCISE: Measure of Uncertainty Tolerance

The following statements (based on the twenty-seven items on the Intolerance of Uncertainty Scale by Freeston et al. 1994) describe people's reactions to uncertainty in daily living. Use the three-point scale to indicate how well each statement describes you by circling the number associated with each statement.

Uncertainty Statements	Does Not Describe Me	Describes Me Somewhat	Accurately Describes Me
Being surprised by an event upsets me greatly.	0	1	2
I get frustrated when I don't have all the information I need.	0	1	2
I like to plan ahead so I can avoid surprises.	0	1	2
Even a small unforeseen development can spoil everything, even when I've done my best planning.	0	1	2
I always want to know what will happen to me in the future.	0	1	2
I can't stand surprises.	0	1	2
I try to organize everything before it happens.	0	1	2
Uncertainty interferes with my ability to live a full life.	0	1	2
I can become paralyzed by uncertainty when making a decision or taking action.	0	1	2
I do not function well when faced with uncertainty.	0	1	2
I try to avoid uncertain situations if at all possible.	0	1	2

If you scored 2 for five or more items, you likely are moderately to highly intolerant of uncertainty. Additional items scored 1 would push your IU score even higher. This measure is intended to give you a sense of your intolerance of uncertainty. More accurate, standardized measures are available in scientific journals (see Buhr and Dugas 2002; Carleton et al. 2007).

If you had a fairly high score, IU is likely an important cause of your problems with doubt. You'll find the treatment strategies in chapter 10 especially helpful in strengthening your tolerance of uncertainty. But for now, in the following sections let's take a closer look at what makes uncertainty so difficult for people with high IU.

Uncertainty Triggers

We experience uncertainty when we confront situations, problems, or issues in the real world. But situations differ in their ability to cause uncertainty. Even people with a high IU are not constantly in a state of doubt. Tiffany, for example, rarely struggled with doubt at work. She had been working the same job for many years and knew it well. There were few surprises. Everything moved along in a fairly predictable manner. But her responsibilities at home were entirely different. It seemed like new problems and issues arose on a daily basis, leaving Tiffany in a state of uncertainty. Whether or not to send her son to a private school was one of them. There was also whether to buy or repair her car, whether to schedule a doctor's appointment about her bouts of nausea, and whether to confront her husband about his careless spending.

> Personally significant situations that are novel, ambiguous, and potentially disruptive are potent triggers of uncertainty.

Situations that are novel, ambiguous, and uncommon have more unknowns than situations that are familiar, predictable, and less complicated. Situations that are perceived as a personal threat and potential life disruption will be more uncertain (Freeston et al. 2020). If you have a high IU, then you will find threatening, novel, and ambiguous situations more distressing. Your "uncertainty detector" will go off, causing you to experience significant doubt and distress. Tiffany found the issues at home more distressing because their significance and novelty elicited more uncertainty than the highly familiar and predictable work environment. Use the following worksheet to list significant, novel, and potentially disruptive situations that have considerable unknowns.

EXERCISE: List of Uncertainty Triggers

Consider the problems, issues, concerns, or situations you are currently facing. Think about what's happening at work or school, in intimate relationships, with parenting, with friendships, with extended family, with your health, with your spirituality or faith, and so forth. In the first column describe three situations associated with at least some uncertainty. In the second column list what is novel, ambiguous, threatening, and disruptive about that situation. An example from Tiffany's experience is provided in the first row.

Uncertainty Situation (Trigger)	What Is Novel, Ambiguous, Threatening, and Disruptive About the Situation?
Our finances are tight; I need to talk to my husband about his excessive online spending.	• We never discuss finances. • I don't know what to say or how to approach him. • He could get very angry and defensive. • I could be walking on eggshells for weeks or months after; it would make home life so tense.

Uncertainty Situation (Trigger)	What Is Novel, Ambiguous, Threatening, and Disruptive About the Situation?

If you had difficulty listing uncertain situations, review the situations you listed in the Doubts About Past Actions and Decisions exercise in the introduction. There will be considerable overlap between the two lists. Also, you can monitor what happens over the next two to three weeks and record any uncertain situations you encounter.

Uncertainty Distress and Arousal

You may be wondering why you have such difficulty with uncertainty. Research on IU indicates that the distress associated with uncertainty is what makes it so intolerable (Freeston et al. 2020). In addition, when an uncertain situation is considered a significant personal threat, we experience greater emotional arousal (muscle tension, feeling keyed up and on edge, restlessness), which can cause considerable distress for high-IU people (Knowles and Olatunji 2023).

It is the distress caused by uncertainty that makes it so intolerable.

Waiting for the results of a medical test can be anxiety provoking. If you're a high-IU person, the wait will be the most distressing part because you will be imagining the worst outcome, which will cause you to feel very keyed up. A person with low IU will find the wait less distressing because they aren't assuming the worst news, so they won't be as keyed up. Take a few minutes to consider your level of distress when facing uncertain situations.

EXERCISE: Uncertainty Distress

Review the doubt situations you listed in the Doubts About Past Actions and Decisions exercise in the introduction and the uncertainty situations you listed in the preceding exercise. Note these experiences in the first column. Beside each experience circle the number that best describes how upset or distressed you feel when you think about the experience.

Doubt/Uncertainty Situations	Not at All Distressing	Quite Distressing	Very Distressing
1.	0	1	2
2.	0	1	2
3.	0	1	2
4.	0	1	2
5.	0	1	2

Does thinking about most of these situations leave you feeling very distressed? This suggests that distress may be an important factor in why you find uncertainty—that is, the unknown—so difficult to handle. In chapter 10 you'll learn about interventions for reducing uncertainty distress.

Uncertainty Beliefs

What you believe about uncertainty has a significant impact on its tolerability. If you believe that uncertainty is a harbinger of negative outcomes, that it should be avoided or at least minimized, and that the best solution for it is to be able to anticipate every conceivable outcome, then uncertainty will feel intolerable. On the other hand, if you believe that uncertainty is no more likely to be associated with negative outcomes than positive ones, and that you're able to deal with whatever comes your way, then you're likely to find uncertainty more tolerable. Uncertainty will not be a threat. Instead, you'll see it as an opportunity to embrace the inevitable unknownness of life. The following measure provides an opportunity for you to determine what you believe about uncertainty.

EXERCISE: The Uncertainty Belief Measure

The following statements reflect beliefs and attitudes about uncertainty. Use the scale beside each item to indicate your level of agreement or disagreement.

Belief Statements	Totally Disagree	Somewhat Disagree	Neither	Somewhat Agree	Totally Agree
1. Uncertain situations are more likely to have a negative outcome.	-2	-1	0	+1	+2
2. I am poor at coping with the unknown and unexpected.	-2	-1	0	+1	+2
3. It's important to organize and plan everything in advance to the best of my ability.	-2	-1	0	+1	+2
4. Even a small unforeseen aspect of a situation can ruin an outcome.	-2	-1	0	+1	+2
5. The unexpected can cause me greater harm than the expected.	-2	-1	0	+1	+2
6. Uncertainty should be avoided or at least minimized.	-2	-1	0	+1	+2

Belief Statements	Totally Disagree	Somewhat Disagree	Neither	Somewhat Agree	Totally Agree
7. Being uncertain makes me more vulnerable.	-2	-1	0	+1	+2
8. It's not fair that life is full of uncertainties.	-2	-1	0	+1	+2
9. Good things can come from the unexpected.	-2	-1	0	+1	+2
10. A person has to be ready to manage the unexpected.	-2	-1	0	+1	+2
11. The unknown is an opportunity for personal growth because it promotes interest, curiosity, and resourcefulness.	-2	-1	0	+1	+2
12. Being spontaneous and taking some risk is necessary even in the face of uncertainty.	-2	-1	0	+1	+2

Items 1 through 8 are negative beliefs about uncertainty, whereas items 9 through 12 are positive beliefs. If you scored in the plus range for the first eight items and in the minus range for the last four, then your beliefs about uncertainty are likely to contribute to feelings of distress and intolerability. However, scores in the minus range for the first eight items and plus scores for the last four suggest your belief system about uncertainty makes it tolerable and not at all distressing.

Coping with Uncertainty

Tiffany was concerned about finances. She and her husband were living paycheck to paycheck and falling behind in some monthly payments. Her husband wanted to apply for a consolidation loan through a bank, but Tiffany was torn. *Would it just drive them further into debt? Was this the best way to deal with their strained finances? Would it give her husband license to spend more?* She found all this uncertainty, the unanswered questions, highly distressing. And so she procrastinated, saying she needed more time to research

> Efforts to curb uncertainty distress can have the unintended effect of making you more aware of uncertainty and the possibility of an undesirable outcome.

the pros and cons of a consolidation loan. But the indecision and avoidance only made matters worse. The longer she procrastinated, the more anxious and distressed she felt as a result of her husband's pressure.

If uncertainty causes you distress, you'll likely try to minimize or avoid it as much as possible. Unfortunately, many of the strategies that reduce uncertainty distress in the short term are less effective in the long term. People use two types of strategies to try and cope with uncertainty distress. They use *overengagement strategies* to try to gain a greater degree of certainty and *underengagement strategies* in an attempt to avoid uncertain situations (Freeston et al. 2020). When facing an uncertain situation, which type of strategy do you tend to use? The next exercise will help you find out.

EXERCISE: Uncertainty Response Checklist

Place a checkmark beside the overengagement and underengagement strategies you tend to use when confronted with a personally significant uncertain situation. .

Overengagement Strategies

☐   I tend to overprepare in an effort to be more certain of an outcome.

☐   I tend to ask lots of questions.

☐   I search for more and more information.

☐   I seek advice and reassurance from others.

Underengagement Strategies

☐   I make a rather quick, impulsive decision.

☐   I dither and am hesitant to choose between different options.

☐   I try to avoid by procrastinating.

☐   I distract myself with other activities to avoid dealing with an uncertain situation.

☐   I avoid gathering information relevant to an uncertain situation.

☐   I flip-flop by switching between different options.

What did you discover about your way of coping with uncertainty? Are you more of an overengagement or underengagement person? Regardless, these strategies are counterproductive because they are attempts to minimize uncertainty. The alternative is to directly engage with the inevitable uncertainty of daily living. Of course, doing so is more difficult if you are distressed by uncertainty and find dealing with the unknown intolerable. Learning a different way to approach uncertainty is one of the chief aims of this workbook.

Wrap-Up

If we could be certain about everything in life, there would be no doubt. But of course, we experience a lot of uncertainty regarding our actions and decisions of the past, as well as for what we will face in the future. It is within the fertile soil of uncertainty that doubt springs forth eternal. Our relationship to uncertainty determines the intensity of our doubt. Those who have an uneasy relationship with uncertainty are at the greatest risk for excessive doubt because uncertainty becomes intolerable when people hold unrealistic beliefs about certainty that cause them to react to unfamiliar, potentially threatening situations in ineffective ways. The elevated distress then fuels further doubt about the situation they face and their ability to cope with it.

In this chapter you learned about the different processes that are feeding your troubled relationship with uncertainty. Becoming more tolerant, more comfortable with uncertainty, is the key to overcoming excessive doubt. Chapter 10 presents interventions for improving your relationship with uncertainty. But for now, let's continue with our exploration of excessive doubt. The next chapter delves into the problem of indecision, which is both a cause and consequence of doubt.

CHAPTER 2

Paralyzed by Indecision

Life is full of decisions. If we want to get technical, every moment of our existence involves a decision. For example, I'm seated at my desk writing these words. *Should I continue to write, or should I get up, move around, and take a break?* In the process of this thought the idea of food pops into my mind. *Am I feeling hungry, or should I ignore the thought?* And if I decide to act on the thought, *Should I venture to the cupboard or the refrigerator? Should I or shouldn't I snack? What should I eat? I'm on a diet but I really want to snack on chips. Should I have just a few chips, or should I resist the temptation?* As you can see, in this sliver of time a whole series of decision making was set in motion. If we think of decision making from this perspective, we make hundreds of decisions every day.

But of course, not all decisions are of equal importance. Some issues requiring a decision are much more important than others. Deciding whether to commit to a long-term relationship, which program to take in college, whether or not to take a course of treatment after a malignant tumor is discovered, or whether to stay or leave a difficult romantic relationship are the types of decisions that cause a period of indecision for most because they have life-changing implications. There are also decisions of an intermediate degree of difficulty that can be more challenging for some than others. For example, when deciding whether to give their opinion in a meeting if they know others might object, what gifts to purchase for a wedding or anniversary, which restaurant

> Deciding what to do, what to say, or how to respond is a fundamental aspect of living. Hardly an hour passes that doesn't require some form of decision making.

to choose for a night out with friends, or what to wear for a special occasion, most people might experience a brief moment of indecision and hesitation but soon take a course of action. For others, these decisions can induce a kind of paralysis.

If decision making is an inherent part of living, and most people experience times of indecision, you might wonder how you'll know if indecision has become a problem. Start your inquiry by answering the three questions in the next exercise.

EXERCISE: Reflections on Indecision

Do you often feel anxious, worried, or distressed when having to make a decision? If yes, list some examples.

_____

_____

Has your life been disrupted because of indecision? Have you missed out on opportunities because you couldn't decide? If yes, what opportunities have you missed due to indecision?

_____

_____

Are you more indecisive than your friends, family, and coworkers? Do they seem to effortlessly make decisions when you're paralyzed by indecision? If yes, what decisions have they made effortlessly that you struggle to make?

_____

_____

If you answered yes to these questions, it is likely that indecision has become a significant problem for you. Were you able to think of several examples of your indecision? Maybe you've noticed that your indecision is getting worse so that several times a day you feel torn, not knowing what to do, full of doubts. If so, this chapter is for you, someone who is often *paralyzed by indecision*. In it we'll take a close look at what causes indecision. Its worksheets and assessment tools will help you determine if these processes are contributing to your indecision. This chapter is the foundation for the interventions described in chapter 11 that will show you how to reduce doubt and become more decisive. Let's first look at how indecision affected Toby.

Toby's Story: *Chronic Indecision*

Toby had never liked making decisions. Even as a child he looked to his friends to decide what to play or who should do what when they played. His other siblings always decided what they would watch, and his parents kept him on a fairly rigid schedule. As he got older, Toby had great difficulty making decisions for himself. In his last year of high school he felt perpetually anxious and worried about what he'd do after graduation. He had good grades and moderately high test scores, so various options were available to him, but he could not make up his mind. He ended up taking a gap year, staying at home and working a couple of part-time jobs. Unfortunately the year off didn't provide any answers, so Toby stayed home and enrolled in the local junior college.

After college Toby got a job in a call center. As a young adult he continued to struggle with indecision. He performed his work reasonably well as long as the calls involved typical problems that fell within his job description. However, the more unusual calls threw him for a loop, and he often hesitated and failed to end the call with a reasonable resolution. On several occasions this got him in trouble with a caller who then lodged a complaint.

Indecision affected Toby's personal life too. He had been dating the same woman for several years but couldn't decide whether to take the relationship to another level of commitment. He thought about going back to college but couldn't decide. He hadn't had a vacation in a couple of years because he couldn't decide where to go or what to do.

Indecision also affected Toby's daily life. He rarely engaged in conversations with friends or coworkers because he wasn't sure what to say, so he came across as aloof and unfriendly. He always waited for others to decide where to dine out, what movie to see, or whether to go to a concert or sports event. He had saved a considerable amount of money but couldn't decide how to invest it, so it sat in a savings account.

In sum Toby's life was significantly limited by his indecision. You could say he was *paralyzed by indecision* and often experienced doubt, anxiety, and worry.

There are many reasons for Toby's indecisiveness. He lacked self-confidence, he was frightened of making a bad decision, he didn't like taking responsibility, and it felt safer to do nothing rather than choose a course of action. He was driven more by a fear of making a wrong decision than a concern about making the best decision. He also held the erroneous belief that he could avoid decision making altogether. In reality, deciding to not take action is itself a decision. So, Toby was only deluding himself by thinking he was not making a decision when he sat tight and did nothing. But one thing was for certain—because of his indecision, Toby was not flourishing. And the many decisions he had to face placed him in a perpetual state of doubt.

When Indecision Is Excessive

You may have a clear sense that your experience of indecision is excessive. One of my clients with OCD had such a severe problem with indecision that he would stand outside the door to my office building waiting for someone to tell him he could enter. He was racked with anxiety and doubt, repeating to himself, "Is it okay to go in or not?" He could not make up his mind on his own. This is a clear example of excessive indecision, but for you maybe the bouts of indecision are not so clear-cut. You may be wondering if your indecision is normal or excessive.

To answer the question, we must explore the distinction between "indecision" and "indecisiveness." Decision making starts with having to choose between two or more options. "Indecision" is the act of not being able to decide on a particular course of action, like having difficulty making a decision about your career. "Indecisiveness" describes a person who has difficulty making decisions for a wide range of life situations, whether they are of great personal significance or not. It describes a personality characteristic associated with low self-confidence, a heightened sense of helplessness, and possibly a great deal of ambivalence (Germeijs and De Boeck 2002). Clearly "excessive indecision" refers to "indecisiveness" and describes a person who has difficulty making decisions in many areas of life—from choosing a movie to deciding whether to commit long term in an intimate relationship. Regardless of the personal significance of the decision or the consequences thereof, the indecisive person wavers, and this wavering is a defining characteristic of excessive indecision.

> The indecisive person exhibits impaired decision making for a wide range of life situations regardless of their significance or consequence.

Maybe you already know that you're an indecisive person. Perhaps close friends or family members have made this observation. Most of us have some idea of how well we handle decision making. Regardless, I recommend you take the indecisiveness measure in the next exercise to determine whether excessive indecision is a problem for you.

EXERCISE: Measure of Indecisiveness

For the following list of statements about making decisions, check true or false to indicate whether the statement describes you or not.

Indecisiveness Items	True	False
In most situations I find it difficult to make decisions.		
I am slower than most at making decisions.		
I often feel at a loss when trying to make a decision.		
I have a strong sense of uncertainty when trying to make a decision.		
I try to put off making a decision for as long as I can.		
I feel anxious, stressed, or worried when trying to make a decision.		
I have difficulty making a decision even with the trivial things in my life.		
I am especially worried about making the wrong decision.		
I often have regrets after making a decision.		
I prefer for someone else to make the decision.		
I often think that my decisions will lead to a negative outcome.		
I prefer to make no decision rather than take decisive action.		
I tend to find the responsibility of making a decision overwhelming.		
I tend to overthink the pros and cons when making a decision.		

Did you have difficulty with the indecisiveness measure? Often people who are indecisive find true or false measures difficult because they are forced to make a decision. If you checked true for seven or more items, consider whether you might be an indecisive person. These results indicate that you tend to experience excessive indecision in many situations, from the mundane to the truly significant. And this indecision causes you to doubt yourself and feel anxious about many life situations. Left unchecked, doubt and indecision can paralyze you, and even cause feelings of discouragement and despair.

There is good news! You don't have to live paralyzed by indecision. In the following sections you'll learn about the root causes of indecisiveness. You'll need these insights before you can use the intervention strategies for indecision in chapter 11.

The Information Gap

We don't make decisions in a vacuum. Instead, we seek information, to varying degrees based on the importance of the decision, to make the best possible choice of action. To do this we need to have some confidence in the accuracy of what we see, hear, read, remember, and understand, as well as know when we have enough information to reach a decision. There is evidence that people who are indecisive have less confidence in their decisions and require more information before reaching a decision than decisive people (Rassin et al. 2007).

> Indecisive people make decisions slower because they require more information and may have less trust in what they see, hear, or remember.

Consider the following example. Imagine you're single and in your mid-twenties. You're stuck in a job that you greatly dislike and has no future. The pay is okay but not great. You are thinking about quitting and going back to school. What should you do?

We can agree that this is a very important decision with life-long implications. You wouldn't want to rush into your decision. There's a lot to consider, and so you seek out multiple sources of information. You read up on what various educational programs have to offer, you calculate the costs and how to deal with the lost income, you seek advice from others, and the like. But at some point you make a decision to stay or go back to school. An indecisive person might put off the decision for months, or even years, thinking they need more information. The decisive person quickly comes to the realization that they have enough information, they can trust what they heard and their ability to think through the options, and that it's time to get off the fence. A decision is made.

But there's one other difference. The indecisive person thinks time is on their side, that a decision can be put off indefinitely, whereas the decisive person has a better understanding of time. When making decisions, are you more like the decisive or indecisive person? The next exercise will help you reflect on your informational demands when making decisions.

EXERCISE: Information Demands in Decision Making

In the space provided write down three decision-making situations from the past. They can range from the more mundane to the very significant. In the second column list what information you had available to help with the decision. In the third column list information you wish you had in your struggle to make a decision. An example from Toby is presented in the first row.

Decision-Making Situation	Information Gathered	Wished-for Information
I can't decide on whether to take a Caribbean vacation this winter.	• Consulted several resort websites • Got detailed info on costs • Got vacation time approved at work • Asked friends about their vacation experiences	• Guarantee of good weather • Know that I'd have a good time • Would meet friendly and interesting people • Would not feel bored or lonely • Return thinking the vacation was well worth the money

Decision-Making Situation	Information Gathered	Wished-for Information

What do you notice about the information you had available and the information you wish you'd had? As you look back on these decision-making situations, is it clear that you really didn't need more information to make the decision? As you can see in Toby's example, the wished-for information was impossible to get. There's no way Toby could have known whether he'd have a good time on vacation or if the weather would be good. Waiting for this most-desired information only prolonged the decision-making process and made him indecisive. Are you avoiding a decision because you erroneously think you need more information, that you can't trust what you already know? Or, like Toby, are you wanting guarantees that are impossible to have?

Tricky Decision-Making Beliefs

What we believe about decision making will determine whether we're a decisive or an indecisive person. I call these "tricky beliefs" because there is some element of truth to each belief. However, if taken too far, the belief turns against you and can cause indecisiveness. This next exercise lists several beliefs about decision making. Take a few minutes to rate your level of agreement or disagreement with each statement.

> Whether you're facing a unique, highly significant decision or you're generally indecisive, what you believe about the decision-making process has a huge impact on your ability to make a decision.

EXERCISE: Decision-Making Belief Scale

Place a checkmark in the column that best describes your level of agreement with each of the twelve beliefs about making a decision.

Belief Statements	Totally Disagree	Somewhat Disagree	Neither	Somewhat Agree	Totally Agree
Most decisions are permanent; they can't be changed later.					
A quick decision is more likely to result in a poor outcome.					
For every decision, there's only one correct option.					
It's important to feel certain that you've made the right decision.					
The more time you take to make a decision, the less likely you are to make a choice you'll later regret.					
Never settle for second best when making a decision.					
You should always have a good feeling about your decisions.					
It's always better to postpone a decision than risk making a less satisfactory decision.					
You should always wait until you have no doubts before deciding what to do.					
Decisions should be as risk free as possible.					
A missed opportunity is more tolerable than a disappointing decision.					
You should always seek the opinion of others before making a decision.					

No doubt you'll agree that these beliefs may be helpful, but they can lead to indecisiveness if taken too far. For example, it's a good idea to *seek the opinion of others before making a decision*, but when do you stop seeking reassurance about the best decision to make? If you feel like you need the advice of more and more people, you'll delay making a decision. The longer the delay, the greater the risk of missing out on a valued opportunity.

To better understand the connection between beliefs and indecisiveness, consider an example from Toby's experience. Toby had a fear of commitment. He had been in a long-term relationship for a couple of years, and his partner had talked about Toby moving in with her, but he dithered, trying to buy time. His indecisiveness was fueled by a number of beliefs: *If I move in, the relationship becomes more permanent and there's no turning back. I need to feel certain I'm making the right decision. It's better to delay a decision than risk a less than satisfactory choice. I need to get more advice and consult with others before making a decision.* It's easy to see from these beliefs why Toby would delay, delay, delay. But relationships have a time limit for delays. The hesitation is a decision and—as happens to so many who fear commitment—Toby's partner ended the relationship. She was done waiting!

If you checked "somewhat agree" or "totally agree" on six or more statements in the preceding exercise, consider whether your beliefs about decision making contribute to your indecisiveness. Some of the interventions in chapter 11 focus on how one can adopt more balanced beliefs about making decisions. In the meantime, use the space below to record beliefs that are especially important contributors to your difficulty in making decisions.

1. _____

2. _____

3. _____

Decision-Making Strategies

The strategies we use to make a decision can promote indecisiveness or make us more effective decision makers. Strategies such as avoidance or being overly focused on reducing emotional distress or discomfort can lead to indecisiveness. In *The Worry Workbook*, Robichaud and Buhr (2018) list seven strategies used in decision making. Many overlap with the engagement and underengagement strategies listed in the Uncertainty Response Checklist (chapter 1), which makes sense because uncertainty contributes to our discomfort with making decisions. Review the decision-making strategies listed below and check those you tend to use most when making a decision.

EXERCISE: Decision-Making Checklist

Place a checkmark beside the strategies you use most often when making decisions.

- ☐   I often ask other people for their opinion on what to do.

- ☐   I gather as much information as possible about my options.

- ☐   I usually try to delay making a decision as long as possible.

- ☐   I often try to get others to make the decision.

- ☐   I try to keep all my options open as long as possible.

- ☐   I prefer to make a quick decision without much consideration.

- ☐   I often flip-flop between various options before settling on a decision.

Can you see how the strategies you checked contribute to your indecisiveness? In chapter 11 you'll be introduced to alternative ways to make decisions that will make you a more efficient decision maker. If you're only occasionally indecisive, changing your approach will be easier than if you're an indecisive person, in which case you'll need a lot more practice and patience to rehabilitate your decision-making skills.

Wrap-Up

Doubt is experienced most forcefully when one is faced with a decision. The greater the personal consequences of a decision, the more intense the doubt. Indecision feeds doubt and vice versa. If you're an indecisive person, you likely experience more frequent and intense doubt. Becoming a more efficient decision maker is a pathway to overcoming excessive doubt.

As you saw in this chapter, there are three reasons why people are indecisive: they put off making a decision because they feel they need more information, they hold extreme beliefs about decision making, and they use avoidant or ill-conceived coping strategies when trying to make a decision. And so, the indecisive person delays much longer than necessary. The delay causes heightened anxiety, worry, and stress about what to do and increases the risk of missed opportunities. This, in turn, intensifies the experience of doubt because doubt and indecision are inextricably connected. The presence of doubt hinders decision-making ability while the person who is indecisive is more likely to experience crippling doubt. This dynamic relationship between doubt and indecision is affected by another process. The inability to achieve a sense of conviction concerning the best course of action can leave us in a quandary and a state of indecision. We'll now turn to this important contributor to doubt.

CHAPTER 3

The Pursuit of Conviction

Have you taken time to reflect on your personal convictions, the strongly held beliefs or values that guide how you live? These beliefs are focused on morality, ethics, and spirituality. They define who we are and how we relate to others. But when doubt creeps into our moral and religious belief system, it can cause a personal crisis. Have you had moments of crisis when you questioned long-held moral or spiritual beliefs?

We speak of having a *firm conviction* when stating our commitment to certain moral and religious values. To uphold these values we subscribe to a set of absolutes with an intense sense of internal certainty regardless of the circumstance and with no room for doubt. What do I mean? Imagine you're at the self-serve checkout: you scan your items, pay, and leave the store. When you get to your car, you realize there's an item you didn't scan. Do you go back in the store and pay for the item or leave for home? If you have a strong conviction for honesty, you'll go back in the store with the unpaid item. If your conviction for honesty isn't so strong, you'll head home with the unpaid item.

We need a strong sense of conviction if we hope to live by our moral and religious beliefs. But when we demand of ourselves a perfect sense of conviction that we're making the right decision or taking the correct course of action—thinking this will settle any doubt—the pursuit of conviction can become another powerful contributor to the problem of doubt.

In this chapter we'll examine why the pursuit of conviction is often not the answer for excessive doubt. Even in the realm of religious or spiritual beliefs, a sense of perfect inner conviction may be an unrealistic expectation. We'll start our discussion by clarifying the difference between "conviction," "belief," and "opinion." We'll then consider three aspects of conviction that make it an inappropriate standard for settling doubts about past actions or decisions: the feeling of knowing, the need for completion, and the search for emotional closure. But before we delve deeper into the topic of conviction, consider Yujin's efforts to deal with her unrelenting doubt.

Yujin's Story: *Searching for Conviction*

Yujin had experienced doubts for as long as she could remember, but they became more prominent after she graduated from college and struck out on her own. She was a conscientious, hardworking professional with a strict moral and ethical code who showed great sensitivity to the needs of others. Yujin's family was highly religious, and in their Christian faith, honesty, integrity, and devotion were sacred trusts. These trusts were absolutes that could not be questioned, and any doubt regarding them was considered an intolerable sin. When she lived at home, Yujin was faithful to her church community and strove to live up to the high ideals of her parents. But she always needed a lot of reassurance when making decisions, and she had doubts that all of her past actions, judgments, and decisions had had the purest of intentions.

Living on her own, Yujin's doubts had intensified and were causing her considerable anxiety and distress. One of the most prominent doubts was a crisis of faith. Yujin had been raised to believe that Christianity was the only path to salvation and a close relationship with God. But meeting good people at work who had different religious beliefs had shaken this conviction, and she had begun to doubt whether Christianity was the only truth. Her inner sense of certainty was gone.

To relieve her distress and regain the lost conviction, Yugin spent hours in online forums and discussion groups that were focused on questions of faith. She expanded her reading in philosophy, theology, and spirituality and consulted with Christian counselors and pastors. She was looking for answers, some truth that would restore that inner sense of conviction, but her effort was futile. Much to her horror, her searching had the opposite effect: her doubts strengthened rather than diminished.

It wasn't only her matters of faith that suffered an onslaught of doubt. Yujin noticed that she was questioning her everyday actions and decisions more so than she had in the past. Even routine tasks such as answering emails became distressing. Yujin prized honesty and kindness, holding firm to the convictions that it is important to tell the whole truth and to not hurt others. One day at work she found herself gripped with doubt about the completeness of her answer to a coworker's question in an email. *Did I leave out details? Was I completely honest? Did I express my opinion tactfully to avoid hurting their feelings?* Yujin knew there was no real answer to these doubts—there would always be some uncertainty—but she felt the need to know that her answer had been right for the occasion. She reread the email, analyzed the coworker's response, but nothing could bring her a sense of conviction. The doubt remained.

Doubt began to affect Yujin's decision making to the point that her productivity suffered. She was working more but accomplishing less. The strain of it all was threatening Yujin's health.

Conviction: A Conundrum for Doubt

Yujin was convinced that conviction was the answer to her doubts. After all, there is no room for doubt when we're convinced of the accuracy, truth, or correctness of our belief, opinion, or action. Conviction involves a deep inner sense of certainty that is not easily swayed by inconsistent evidence, persuasion, or experience. To feel conviction is to *feel* utterly convinced of a particular version of the truth.

To understand conviction, consider one of your core values. Maybe it's the Golden Rule, which is to treat others as you'd like to be treated. You're not entirely sure about the origins of this value, but about it you'd say, "I have a firm conviction in treating others like I'd like to be treated." It's a guiding principle of your life that affects your actions and decisions. It's a self-determined declaration that is not open to persuasion or contradiction. You have no doubts about the truth of the Golden Rule.

> *Conviction* is a deep, internal sense of certainty that is resistant to doubt.

But imagine trying to acquire that same level of conviction when making specific decisions, such as which of two job offers to take. Or what about when trying to allay your doubts about whether you should have acted with more empathy toward a person? How could you possibly attain the same level of certainty—that feeling of conviction—you have for your core values for such things? As you will see, trying to attain firm conviction is not the answer for settling doubts about past actions, decision making, or beliefs that we are now questioning.

> The feeling of conviction is most evident in our moral, ethical, and religious values and articles of faith.

The feeling of conviction is most appropriate for moral, ethical, and religious values. Moral values are our personal standards for right and wrong that guide our behavior and choices. They include our ideas about honesty, integrity, respect, fairness, responsibility, compassion, and forgiveness. Conviction is also evident in the religious sphere; a belief in God or a universal spirit and the existence of an afterlife are examples of such convictions. Conviction in the moral and religious domains also informs our stance on sociopolitical issues such as climate change, gun control, reproductive rights, civil liberties, and the like.

When thinking about conviction in the context of doubt, it's important to make a distinction between opinion, belief, and conviction. The pyramid in the following figure illustrates this distinction. As you move up the pyramid, the strength of belief in an idea becomes less amenable to change.

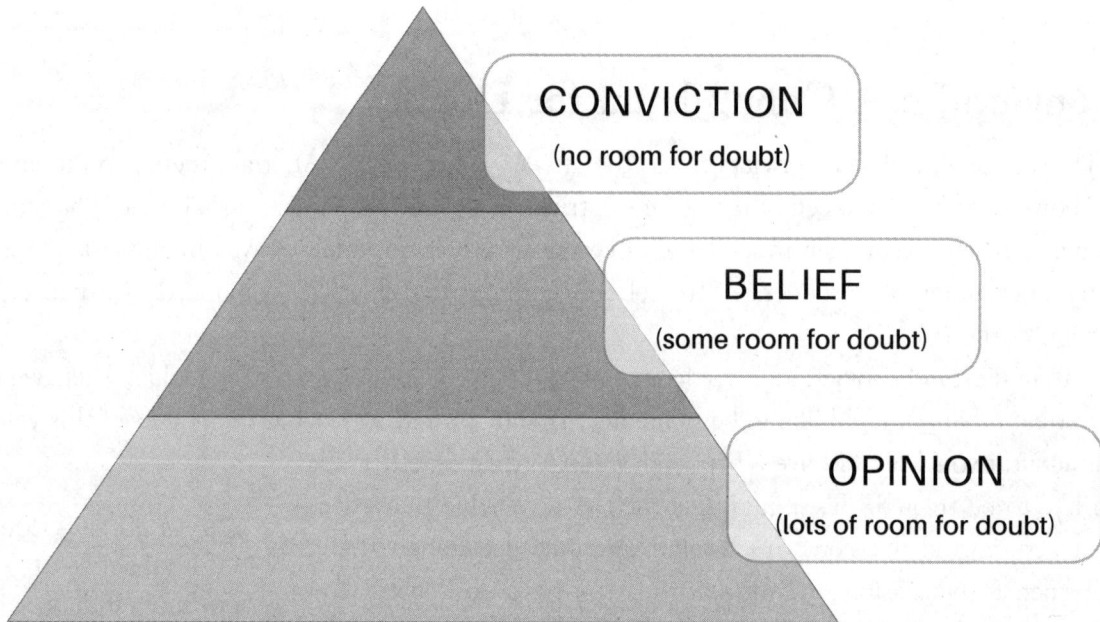

CONVICTION
(no room for doubt)

BELIEF
(some room for doubt)

OPINION
(lots of room for doubt)

Let's start with *opinions*. We all have opinions on a host of topics, such as how to eat healthy, what's the best form of exercise, which football team is most likely to win the Super Bowl, who is the most impactful musician, and so on. We rarely have much personal investment in our opinions, and so we can have considerable doubt about whether we have the correct view. We can be easily persuaded to change an opinion.

Then there are *beliefs*. In the book's introduction, beliefs were defined as mental representations of phenomena in the physical world or as abstractions that we are convinced are true. They are our assumptions about the self, the world, and others. Beliefs provide meaning; they are how we make sense of our existence. And so, we are a great deal more invested in our beliefs. There is less room for doubt and persuasion when it comes to beliefs, although they can change over time and with experience, and we hold some more strongly than others. In other words, we can doubt our beliefs, as Yujin did about the authority of God.

Finally, we have *conviction*, which is a felt sense of certainty that is so strong that there is no room for doubt. People who are struggling with doubt often strive for conviction because they want a felt sense of certainty. For example, let's say you're at work and doubting whether you shut the windows at home before leaving for work that morning. If you could work up a convincing feeling that the windows were shut, then your doubt would vanish. But making yourself feel convinced is extremely difficult, especially when the doubt is strong and unrelenting.

Can you see how the pursuit of conviction is not the answer for excessive doubt about past actions or decisions? This next exercise asks you to reflect more deeply on your moral, ethical, and religious values to get a better understanding of the role conviction plays in your life.

> Striving for internal conviction only aggravates doubt for most types of personal concerns.

EXERCISE: Core Values Checklist

The following is a list of values that help us distinguish right from wrong. Place a checkmark next to only those values that are especially important to you, for which you have an unwavering belief in its truth regardless of the circumstances. A checkmark means you hold to the value with firm conviction.

I have a firm conviction in:

- ☐ **Honesty:** telling the truth even when it is difficult.

- ☐ **Compassion:** being kind and considerate toward others.

- ☐ **Justice:** exercising equality, fairness, and impartial judgment in my interactions with others.

- ☐ **Respect:** recognizing the rights and boundaries of other peoples' perspectives and cultures.

- ☐ **Hard work:** taking responsibility for putting effort into my work and seeing it through to completion.

- ☐ **Virtue:** striving for goodness, uprightness, moral clarity, purity of intention.

- ☐ **Forgiveness:** letting go of unfairness and grudges.

- ☐ **Gratitude:** expressing appreciation for what I have.

- ☐ **Integrity:** being guided by moral values and principles.

- ☐ **Autonomy:** taking initiative with and responsibility for my actions and decisions.

- ☐ **Theology:** believing in the existence of God or a universal spirit.

- ☐ **Hope:** believing in the existence of an afterlife (heaven, hell, and so forth).

- ☐ **Authority:** respecting certain sacred texts as the word of God.

- ☐ **Mystery:** believing that miracles and supernatural phenomena happen.

The values you selected in this exercise are deeply personal. They have developed out of your life experiences, upbringing, education, cultural influences, religious training, and the like. These are your core values, and you hold them with firm conviction. This list is your reference point for understanding your experience of conviction. Next we consider three processes to explain why the feeling of conviction cannot eliminate most forms of excessive doubt.

A Feeling of Knowing

You probably know what the "tip-of-the-tongue" phenomenon is. For example, you have a feeling, an intuitive sense, that you know the name of an acquaintance, but you can't produce the person's name. You feel so close to remembering their name that it's on *the tip of your tongue*, but alas, you're left annoyed and frustrated when you still can't remember the person's name. Clearly you can't say you know the person's name because you can't remember their name, but you have a feeling that you know it. This is an example of a *feeling of knowing* as opposed to a "knowing of knowing."

This feeling of knowing occurs repeatedly in our day-to-day actions. Think of all the things we do in the run of the day, such as speaking, texting, cooking, cleaning, parenting, and so on. We don't doubt our actions—not because our memory of what we said or did is perfect but because we have a feeling of knowing that what we did was done right.

> An internal sense of conviction—that is, a feeling of knowing that *arises naturally*—erases doubt about past actions, decisions, or core beliefs.

This same feeling of knowing guides our decision making and moral choices. You need to decide whether to meet a person you matched with on a dating app, your manager asks you to leave out a detail in your report that makes him look bad, you need to choose which car to buy, your teenage daughter tells you in confidence that your best friend's daughter is using drugs and you need to decide what to do, and so on. In each instance you think through the pros and cons of different choices, but in the end your decision often comes down to a feeling—that X is the right decision.

If you're experiencing intense and persistent doubt about an issue, or if doubt has spread to most areas of your life, it's likely that the *feeling of knowing* is not occurring naturally. This is what happens with people who suffer from OCD. Excessive doubt often drives their obsessions and compulsions because of an inability to acquire a feeling of knowing, or what is also called *subjective conviction* (see Clark 2019). To deal with this deficit of inner conviction, a person with excessive doubt tries to create the feeling of knowing by checking their actions repeatedly to ensure they were done completely and correctly. But checking only makes the doubt worse because it erodes their confidence in their memory, and their recollections of the check become less clear and detailed the more they check. As you can see, repeated checking is rarely helpful in trying to create a feeling of knowing.

Reassurance seeking is another strategy people often use to try and gain greater subjective conviction (that feeling of knowing) for problematic doubt (Seif and Winston 2019). This might involve asking other people whether a past action or decision was correct or endlessly searching the internet for reassuring answers. For example, let's say you've been experiencing nausea regularly and don't know whether to make an appointment with the doctor. You want to believe it's nothing serious and will pass with time, but you have a nagging doubt, and so you ask your spouse, family, and friends for advice, and search the internet for information. None of these efforts bring you a lasting sense of knowing, and instead you're left with considerable anxiety. As you can see, reassurance seeking is another ineffective way to deal with doubt or achieve a sense of inner conviction because any reassurance you receive will not be convincing, and soon you will begin to question what you were told or what you read. The doubt remains and you will need to seek a new round of reassurance from a different source.

> Repeated checking and reassurance seeking will not give you the feeling of knowing that drives away doubt about past actions and decisions.

What if it's not possible to intentionally produce a feeling of knowing when doubt persists over past actions, decisions, judgments, or beliefs? This next exercise focuses on your experience of trying to manipulate the feeling of knowing in two ways: reducing a feeling of knowing when you have a firm conviction in a core value, or creating a feeling of knowing when you have doubt about some action, decision, or belief.

EXERCISE: The Feeling of Knowing

This exercise has two parts. First, review the Core Values Checklist from earlier in the chapter and select two values that you checked. Write them in the first column. Then imagine what you'd have to do or experience for your firm conviction in each value to be diminished and write this in the second column. Use the examples from Yujin to guide you.

Moral/Religious Core Values	Experience That Would Diminish Feeling of Knowing
Honesty; telling the truth	Honesty is a core value, but I might start to question it if I see that dishonesty is always rewarded and honesty is often punished.
Belief in an afterlife	I'm not dissuaded by scientific, rational arguments or the opinions of others. Maybe if I had a near-death experience and remembered nothing, I might then question the existence of an afterlife.

Moral/Religious Core Values	Experience That Would Diminish Feeling of Knowing

Now, review what you wrote in the Doubts About Core Beliefs exercise in the book's introduction and list two of them in the first column below. Next, in the adjacent column write what you'd have to do or experience to produce a certain feeling of knowing that would address your doubt. Again, examples from Yujin are provided.

Doubting Problem	Experience That Would Increase Feeling of Knowing
Was I completely honest when I advised Charlene about how to deal with a conflict she was having with another coworker?	· If I kept going back to Charlene with every new insight that came to me, then I'd feel I was being completely honest. · If I said everything that I knew was true even when I knew it would upset Charlene and could jeopardize our friendship. · If I stopped being reminded of my conversation with Charlene and could forget what I said to her. · If Charlene told me I gave her excellent advice; that she acted on that advice and now the conflict is resolved.
Have I sincerely confessed all my sins and wrongdoings to God and asked for His forgiveness?	· If every time a bad thought pops into my mind, I immediately confess it to God. · If I get emotional and tearful every time I say a confessional prayer. · I feel God's blessing in my life and feel gratitude for His forgiveness every moment of the day. · I feel the Holy Spirit whisper in my inner being.

Doubting Problem	Experience That Would Increase Feeling of Knowing

Did you notice in Yujin's examples how difficult, almost impossible, it would be to create a feeling of knowing that she was completely honest with Charlene or had sincerely confessed all her sins? Similarly, her conviction in the values of honesty and the existence of an afterlife are not easily shaken, so the experiences she'd need to diminish her feeling of knowing would be extreme to say the least. Is this true for the experiences you wrote about? Can you see that trying to manufacture a feeling of knowing is an unrealistic, futile standard for resolving persistent doubt about past actions, decisions, or beliefs? This is the main reason why the pursuit of conviction can't solve excessive doubt.

Search for Completeness and Emotional Closure

Trying to create a feeling of knowing is not the only way people pursue conviction and settle their doubts. Often individuals struggling with doubt are driven to seek a feeling of completeness or emotional closure. The need to obtain completeness is most evident in people with a form of OCD that is concerned with order and symmetry. For example, if they see a picture that is slightly crooked or magazines strewn about on a table, they have a strong urge to straighten the picture or stack the magazines. However, you don't have to suffer from OCD to find yourself searching for completion.

> Trying to create a feeling of knowing is not an effective strategy for instilling conviction and resolving the problem of persistent doubt.

The search for completeness is driven by a difficulty in achieving a desired level of satisfaction in your actions, intentions, or experiences. You simply feel like something is "just not right" (Summerfeldt 2004). The emotional and sensory feedback you process is insufficient for you to achieve a sense of completion. For example, you doubt whether you locked the door when leaving your house because you can't remember if the door shut completely. You can't recall whether you heard the latch catch. Or, you obsess over whether you cut a person off in traffic because you don't have a complete and accurate memory of looking in your side mirror and using your turn signal. It's natural to think you can resolve these doubts by trying hard to recall as much detail as possible so you will have a complete memory of your actions. But inevitably, something will escape you. There will be something you feel unsure about that leaves room for doubt.

> Producing a satisfactory level of feeling complete can be quite elusive and thus a poor strategy for dealing with persistent doubt.

Another example of the need for completeness is the person who can't tell you an abbreviated version of their experience because they have to tell you everything, the complete story, in excruciating detail so it's done just right. But just like the feeling of knowing, creating that just-right feeling or sense of completeness can be exceedingly difficult, if not impossible, when you have excessive doubt. *Did I tell my friend everything that happened? Did I leave anything out? Do they really understand what happened to me?* These doubts result in an exceedingly lengthy rendition of past experiences.

Emotional closure refers to the feeling that a past experience is resolved, understood, or complete (Crawley 2010) and is another concept that is highly relevant to the pursuit of conviction. People believe that if they can achieve emotional closure for a past action or decision, they will stop thinking about the experience. They'd have a sense that they could move on, put the experience behind them, and, of course, not doubt past actions or decisions.

As an example, let's say you're with a small group of friends and tell a risqué joke. A couple of people don't laugh. You get home and can't stop thinking about the experience. *Did I offend them?* You can feel your emotions build and your doubt intensifies. You worry about the consequences and whether this moment threatens your friendship and reputation. You're unable to resolve the doubt, and so you keep going over in your mind what you said and how people reacted. In a bid for closure, you ask a couple of friends who were present whether they thought you were offensive. Unfortunately, their reassurances don't help in your quest for closure.

> The more distressing a doubting experience, the more difficult it is to achieve emotional closure.

The search for completeness and emotional closure are indicators that you're trying to achieve an internal sense of conviction. Unfortunately, when we struggle with doubt, it can be impossible to fully achieve both a feeling of completeness and emotional closure. This next exercise gives you an opportunity to consider how completeness and emotional closure might influence your efforts to deal with problematic doubt.

EXERCISE: Your Search for Completeness and Emotional Closure

Select two of the most significant doubting concerns you listed in the Doubts About Past Actions and Decisions, Experiences of Indecision, or the Doubts About Core Beliefs exercises in the book's introduction and write them in the space provided. Next, write down what would have to happen for you to achieve a feeling of completeness that would ease your doubt. What information or proof would you need to feel complete? Then briefly explain what you'd need to experience to have a sense of emotional closure. Your answers should be the *perfect* completeness or emotional closure that would address your doubts. Use the example from Yujin to guide you.

Doubting concern: *I'm getting indications from Kwan that he's wanting a deeper level of commitment; I don't know whether I want to make a commitment or break it off.*

1. What would give you a sense of completeness?

   If I could be more fully aware of the time I spend with Kwan, be completely attentive to his conversation, be more completely interested in his life, that might be a way to tell that I'm ready to make a deeper commitment to this relationship.

2. What would give you a feeling of emotional closure?

   Throughout the day I would be thinking about my times with Kwan and have a deep feeling of happiness and anticipation for our next date. I would have only positive feelings when remembering my time with Kwan and I would feel that he is the right person for me.

Doubting concern: _____

_____

    1.   What would give you a sense of completeness?

       _____

       _____

    2.   What would give you a feeling of closure?

       _____

       _____

Doubting concern: _____

_____

    1.   What would give you a sense of completeness?

       _____

       _____

    2.   What would give you a feeling of closure?

       _____

       _____

What do you notice about Yujin's answers? Her doubts about her romantic relationship suggest a fear of commitment. Should she continue seeing Kwan knowing the relationship is getting more serious, or should she break it off? But notice that what she needs to have a sense of completeness and emotional closure is totally unrealistic. There is no way she can ever meet these standards, so as long as she holds on to them, she won't be able to overcome her doubt. There will be no conviction for which decision is right.

Did you notice the same dilemma with your answers? Are the criteria for feeling a sense of completeness or emotional closure so high that you will never be successful? Because completeness or emotional closure (or both) are unattainable, you're left with your doubt and a lack of conviction over your actions, decisions, or beliefs. A feeling of incompleteness and lack of closure would persist along with your doubt.

Wrap-Up

One way to resolve excessive doubt is to feel a firm conviction that your past actions and decisions were satisfactory, or that your decision making is sound. But as we have seen, pursuing conviction is an ineffective strategy for dealing with doubt because the feeling of knowing, completeness, and emotional closure, all core features of conviction, are difficult to produce. You won't be able to use more effective interventions that are presented in later chapters until you're convinced that pursuing a sense of conviction is not the answer for doubt. In the meantime, we'll turn to another psychological process that makes doubt worse: striving for perfection.

CHAPTER 4

The Perfect Solution

Are you a perfectionist? If so, you're not alone. Perfectionism is a common personality trait and one that may be on the rise (Curran and Hill 2019). There's a strong connection between perfectionism and psychological problems such as anxiety, depression, and possibly OCD (Lunn et al. 2023). And doubt plays an important role in perfectionism. Perfectionism is complicated because there is more than one type, and it can be healthy or unhealthy depending on what you mean by perfectionism.

It's not hard to see why perfectionists might experience high levels of distressing doubt. People with unhealthy perfectionism base their self-worth on striving to attain unreasonably high and inflexible performance standards, have a fear of making mistakes, and have a tendency for excessive self-criticism (Egan et al. 2014; Stoeber and Otto 2006). For these individuals, curbing perfectionism is a necessary prelude to working on excessive doubt. The good news is that an effective cognitive behavioral treatment protocol has been developed specifically for clinical (that is, unhealthy) perfectionism (Shafran et al. 2023). In this chapter we'll focus specifically on the relationship between unhealthy perfectionism and doubt.

This chapter begins by considering the difference between perfectionistic striving and what has been termed *excellencism* (Gaudreau et al. 2022). In this chapter you'll find assessment tools for determining which concept is most relevant for you. We'll then consider how adherence to unrealistic performance standards and excessive self-criticism contribute to the problem of self-doubt. A

> Perfectionists derive their self-worth from striving to attain unrealistic goals for which even minor mistakes are intolerable.

final section examines the relationship between low memory confidence and doubts about past actions and decisions.

Let's begin with the following case example that illustrates how perfectionism fuels doubt, especially for someone with an obsessive-compulsive personality. If you already know that you're a perfectionist, or if this chapter leads you to believe perfectionism is a problem for you, consider also exploring these helpful resources: *When Perfect Isn't Enough* (Antony and Swinson 2009) and *Overcoming Perfectionism* (Shafran et al. 2018).

Charlotte's Story: *A "Perfect" Path to Doubt*

Charlotte had a reputation for meticulousness. Her apartment was immaculate with everything arranged in a neat and orderly fashion. She couldn't stand anything being out of place. She was forever cleaning and tidying up her apartment. Charlotte was a "details" person and so was very well suited to her job as an insurance claims clerk. Her main responsibility was reviewing insurance claims and other documents to make sure everything had been completed correctly. Charlotte was a dedicated, hardworking employee with a reputation for reliability and conscientiousness. As a single woman in her mid-forties with few friends and a distant relationship with her family, her job was one of the few outlets that gave her a sense of self-worth and value. But Charlotte had to have things done her way, and this inflexible and uncompromising stance frustrated her coworkers.

> Unhealthy perfectionism is often a major contributor to doubts about self-worth and the correctness of past actions and decisions.

Charlotte's pathway to doubt ran straight through her perfectionism. Her high standards of performance and expectation of flawlessness gave her many opportunities to doubt herself. *Have I caught all the mistakes in this document? Did I correctly understand what I've read? Am I meeting my manager's expectations? What if I overlooked something? I'd never live with myself knowing I'd made a mistake.* These perfectionistic demands meant that Charlotte was continually in a state of doubt. They also led to much self-criticism, especially when she made a mistake or failed to meet a standard. Because she expected nothing less than 100 percent from herself, she was much slower to complete her work than others. Self-doubt caused her to compulsively check her work until she had the feeling that she could let it go.

Self-doubt was not Charlotte's only issue. She also struggled with obsessive doubt regarding past actions and decisions, such as wondering if she accidentally cut off another car on her way to work or worrying that she'd be late for an appointment because she stayed too long at work. Charlotte often doubted the actions she took and the decisions she made during the day. The doubt was driven by her high standards and expectations, her efforts to achieve a flawless performance, a desire to maintain control and be correct, and a tendency toward excessive self-criticism when she fell short of perfection.

Does Charlotte's story sound familiar? If so, your problem with doubt may be due to perfectionism. Maybe you share some of Charlotte's characteristics but you're not sure whether perfectionism is a problem or just an aspect of your personality. The next section should help answer this question. We begin with an explanation of the difference between excellencism and unhealthy perfectionism.

Perfectionism or Excellencism?

It is obvious that not all perfectionism is unhealthy. Striving to be our best is commendable and can motivate us to accomplish great things. After all, success is one aspect of flourishing. It contributes to a full and satisfying life. We have a great debt of gratitude to the host of perfectionists through the ages who wouldn't settle for second best. Thomas Edison, for example, conducted thousands of experiments before discovering a viable filament for the incandescent lightbulb.

And yet, over the years I've seen many clients whose perfectionism was extreme and caused them significant personal distress, severely limiting their ability to function. In some instances, they were so ensnared by unrealistic standards and a desire for flawlessness that they couldn't perform even the most basic functions of daily living. So, there are clearly two types of perfectionism, the one leading to success and flourishing and the other to despair and defeat.

Excellencism

The pursuit of high-performance standards is healthy if it results in excellence. Psychologist Patrick Gaudreau coined the term *excellencism* and defines it as "a tendency to aim and strive toward very high yet attainable standards in an effortful, engaged, and determined yet flexible manner" (2019, 200). Words like "competent," "productive," "success-ful," and "capable" describe the person who strives for excellence. Gaudreau (2019) notes two other important characteristics of excellencism. In the pursuit of excellence, goals should be specific, clear, and attainable with a well-conceived implementation plan. Also, the person striving for excellence should know when to stop. They should know when they've reached the point of diminishing returns where more time and effort will yield little gain.

> Striving for excellence enables us to reach our full potential.

To understand how excellencism works, imagine you're taking final exams either in high school or college. You have several courses, and some are harder than others. You're struggling with calculus, so you're spending lots of time preparing for that exam, but as a result you're not putting as much time into studying for other exams. Are you able to recognize when you've put enough time and effort into calculus? *I'm not going to improve much more; I better move on to the other courses.* The person pursuing excellence, as opposed to perfection, is able to recognize when they've done their best, to stop studying calculus, and to focus their attention on the other courses.

The unhealthy perfectionist is not so strategic. They keep working on calculus because they still don't know the material perfectly, flawlessly, even though they are putting the grades of their other courses in jeopardy. The unhealthy perfectionist's doubt keeps them striving—*I'm not sure I know enough to pass calculus*—whereas the doubt of the excellencist allows them to move on to other courses: *I'll never know for certain that I know enough; I've done my best, and little will be gained by spending more time on the subject.*

In the space provided, write about a time when you pursued excellence and avoided getting trapped in unhealthy perfectionism. But first, consider Charlotte's example.

A couple of years ago, my manager asked me to review a very complex application made by an important client. I was very busy at the time, so I couldn't spend a huge amount of time on it. But I did my best and found several inconsistencies. I got a commendation from senior management because my work saved the company a lot of money.

Unhealthy Perfectionism

Unhealthy perfectionism goes well beyond doing your best. It is characterized by a relentless striving to attain an idealized, flawless, and excessively high standard (Gaudreau 2019). You are overly concerned about making mistakes, you doubt your actions and decisions, and you believe you must attain unrealistically high standards that you believe others expect of you (Stoeber and Otto 2006). People with unhealthy perfectionism also experience a greater discrepancy between actual performance and their high expectations, creating opportunity for intense self-criticism.

> Perfectionists are rarely successful in meeting their unrealistic expectations, so failure is inevitable.

You can probably see how unhealthy perfectionism would play out in our exam scenario. The perfectionistic person quickly feels overwhelmed by the prospect of preparing for multiple exams. They hold unrealistic standards of perfect performance for each. They feel compelled to be perfectly prepared for each course before they can study for the next. The material must be studied intensely until it is perfectly memorized and understood thoroughly. The perfectionist repeatedly tests their calculus knowledge, and when they fall short they go back and study the material over and over. Inevitably they reach the point of diminishing returns where more time and effort yield little improvement. Their failure to recognize this point means they sacrifice time on other course material to attain perfection with calculus. As the exam date looms closer, the perfectionistic individual experiences intense anxiety and worry. They realize they've overprepared for one course and neglected the rest and yet feel helpless to change course.

Does this exam dilemma sound familiar? Do you overprepare for one task because of perfectionistic strivings, thereby neglecting others? In the space below briefly describe an experience of unhealthy perfectionistic striving. First, consider Charlotte's example.

I invited several coworkers for a social event at my house. I was really anxious about doing this because I'm not a sociable person. I spent so much time cleaning and organizing my apartment perfectly that I didn't have enough time to prepare tasty appetizers. I ended up with a few store-bought snacks. I could tell people were disappointed with the inadequate party food. I felt so embarrassed and inadequate.

_____

_____

_____

_____

_____

_____

Do you have a tendency to pursue excellence or unrealistic perfectionism? Of course, some people are nonperfectionists. They don't have high-performance standards and lack a drive to achieve (Gaudreau 2019). But this is not necessarily a better approach to life given our competitive, success-driven society. Instead, a moderate level of excellencism might be optimal for healthy living. Rather than categorize yourself as an excellencist or a perfectionist, it might be better to think of these characteristics on a continuum in which you are more or less of one or the other. The following exercise (based on a measure developed by Gaudreau et al. 2022) is useful for determining where you lie on this continuum.

EXERCISE: Assessment of Excellencism and Perfectionism

In the list below there are eight characteristics of excellencism on the left and of perfectionism on the right. Place an X on the line to indicate whether you tend toward excellencism or perfectionism. The line represents a continuum; an X in the middle suggests that you are unsure how to rate yourself, whereas an X all the way to the right or left indicates you identify strongly with perfectionism or excellencism, respectively.

1. I work toward high goals or standards of performance.	_____	I strive toward perfect performance.
2. I can accept mistakes and learn from them.	_____	I must avoid making mistakes; they are intolerable.
3. I strive to be competent and productive.	_____	I strive to be exceptionally competent and productive.
4. I set my own goals and standards.	_____	I must set higher standards for myself than others.
5. I work hard and most often produce high-quality work.	_____	I work relentlessly until I feel I've attained perfection.
6. I often feel challenged by my goals and standards.	_____	I often feel overwhelmed by my goals and standards.

7. I am not intimidated by a difficult task; I know I can work through it.			Difficult tasks make me more doubtful that I'll succeed to my satisfaction.
8. I often achieve my goals or meet my expectations.			I rarely achieve my goals or meet my expectations.

If you placed most of your *X*'s toward the left side of the line, then excellencism is most relevant for you. But if most of your ratings were to the right of center, then perfectionism is most applicable. This means it's possible that perfectionism is driving some of your problems with doubt. Next we consider how perfectionism intensifies excessive doubt.

> Excellencism and perfectionism are two different pathways for goal striving.

Perfectionistic Standards and the Rise of Self-Doubt

Imagine you are confronted with a difficult, novel task, and you're not sure what to do. In this moment, you experience uncertainty, questioning your competence and ability to deal with the task at hand. This state of being uncertain about your skills, beliefs, emotions, and decisions is called *self-doubt*. Self-doubt can cause you to question the truth of who you are and your self-worth. In some cases self-doubt manifests itself as *the imposter phenomenon*, in which you feel like a fraud and that people are going to find out who you really are—for example, that you're not as intelligent or knowledgeable as you might appear. And once they find these things out, they'll judge you negatively and not respect you.

It is easy to see how holding perfectionistic performance standards would provide numerous opportunities for you to be disappointed in yourself. Failure can lead to self-criticism, which in turn can fuel a chronic state of self-doubt. For example, say Charlotte is confronted with learning a new software system for keeping track of insurance claims. The training she receives is inadequate and yet she is expected to become proficient in the new system quickly. She feels enormous pressure, which is compounded by her perfectionism. She sets a goal to become flawless with the new system by the end of the week. This is completely unrealistic, and so it's not surprising that by the week's end, Charlotte is still making mistakes. She then

> Self-doubt is a feeling of uncertainty about your capabilities, beliefs, and value. At a deeper level, it may involve questions about your self-identity.

experiences a profound sense of self-doubt because she failed to gain the level of proficiency she expected of herself. She feels so distressed by the whole experience that she seriously thinks about quitting. She's convinced that she's not smart enough to catch on to the new system, and it would be better to quit than to experience the humiliation of continued mistakes.

Like Charlotte, do you often experience self-doubt? Maybe you feel like an imposter and that others will discover your weakness and vulnerability. Are you worried they'll conclude that you don't belong and you'll be forced to leave in disgrace? If you think self-doubt is a problem for you, consider whether unrealistic goals and personal standards are a contributing factor. The next two exercises will help you determine whether you hold unhealthy perfectionistic personal standards that contribute to self-doubt, or whether your beliefs align more readily with healthy excellencism.

EXERCISE: Personal Standard Beliefs Scale

For the following list of belief statements about goal setting and personal standards, circle the number that indicates how much each statement applies to you.

Belief Statements	Don't Agree	Agree a Little	Agree a Lot
It's important that I achieve the highest standards possible.	0	1	2
High goals motivate me to reach my potential and beyond.	0	1	2
Most often I believe I could do better even when I've succeeded.	0	1	2
I must be thoroughly competent in everything I do.	0	1	2
I must strive to be flawless even though I know absolute perfection is impossible.	0	1	2
I need to strive at being exceptional by outperforming others in my comparison group.	0	1	2
I don't settle for less than 100 percent in everything I do.	0	1	2
I expect much more from myself than most people.	0	1	2
I believe in working relentlessly to surpass the goals and expectations set by others.	0	1	2
The pursuit of perfection is the key to success and life fulfillment.	0	1	2

Did you *agree a lot* with many of the belief statements? If so, you may be holding excessively high personal standards that place you in the perfectionism range for personal standards. These beliefs will fuel considerable self-doubt. Because your goals and personal standards are so high, you'll often fail to meet your expectations. This will cause you to question your competence and self-worth, which are the hallmarks of self-doubt.

Maybe you mostly chose *don't agree* because you found the statements too extreme. If so, consider whether the statements in the following exercise are more representative of how you approach goal setting.

EXERCISE: Excellencism Beliefs Scale

Place a checkmark beside the statements that best characterize your attitude about goals and personal standards.

- ☐ It's important that I set high goals and standards.

- ☐ High goals motivate me to perform better.

- ☐ Most of the time I feel satisfied when I've succeeded.

- ☐ I strive to be competent in the important tasks of life.

- ☐ I strive to do my best, knowing that perfection is impossible.

- ☐ Being a productive, skillful person is important to me.

- ☐ I believe that giving 100 percent is not necessary in many of my everyday tasks.

- ☐ I set my own goals without regard to other people's expectations and judgments.

- ☐ It's important that I work hard to reach my goals and personal standards.

- ☐ Achievement is one of several contributors to my sense of worth and life satisfaction.

If you placed a checkmark next to most of these statements, then your goal setting and personal standards are more consistent with excellencism than perfectionism. These more realistic, balanced beliefs are less likely to cause self-doubt.

Charlotte knew that perfectionistic performance beliefs were unhealthy and likely contributing to her self-doubt and criticism. Clearly the excellencism beliefs were the healthy alternative, but

> Striving for unattainable goals will lead to self-doubt, whereas efforts to achieve ambitious yet realistic goals will strengthen self-confidence.

she found she could not shift her perspective. She naturally returned to the more extreme perfectionism beliefs, setting herself up for failure and disappointment. And these results confirmed in her mind that her doubts about her strength and abilities were valid. If, like Charlotte, you have self-doubts, several strategies presented in chapters 9, 10, and 11 can help you shift from holding perfectionistic standards to setting excellencism goals.

A Perfect Memory

How is your memory? Are you quite confident in its accuracy, or do you often doubt your memories of past experiences? It is well-known that memory, a reconstruction of past events and experiences, is biased and inaccurate. This is easily confirmed by recalling a disagreement you had with a family member or friend about something you both heard. You remember hearing one thing, whereas your friend or family member heard something quite different. You both have different memories of the same experience.

Accuracy is not the main issue when it comes to how memory affects doubt. Rather it's the level of confidence you have in your memory that is most critical. No doubt you've met people who are overly confident in the accuracy of their memory. Whatever they remember, that's what actually took place. You can't disagree with a person who's highly confident in their memories. Their motto is, *What I remember is what happened.* They have no doubt about their past actions or judgments.

But then there are people with low memory confidence. Every statement about the past is prefaced with or accompanied by "I think…" If you have low memory confidence, you're not sure that you remember the past accurately. You have significant doubts about past actions and decisions. You think *I don't have a clear memory of shutting the door completely and hearing the dead bolt click, I can't remember signing my name on the last page on my income tax documents before filing them,* or *I don't have a clear image in my mind of marking an X beside my preferred candidate when voting.*

The reality is that we take numerous actions and make many decisions every day, and we have to draw on our memory to dispel our doubts we have about them or to trust that we did something even if we can't perfectly remember it. If your confidence in your memory is low, then you're more likely to doubt what you did in the past.

> Low memory confidence is feeling uncertain that you recall past experiences accurately.

The relationship between memory confidence and doubt is further complicated when perfectionism is thrown into the mix. If you have an impossibly high expectation of being able to clearly and accurately visualize every detail of a past action, your memory confidence will plummet, and doubt will rise. For example, you think, *Did I pack enough snacks for my child's daycare lunch?* You're not sure, and so you search your memory, trying to recall every detail, every step of packing the lunch. If your criteria for accepting your recall are stringent and you can't recall every step, you lose confidence in your recall and doubt creeps in. You conclude by thinking *I don't know, so I better call the daycare so they can check.*

Memory confidence is not all or nothing. There are degrees of memory confidence, as illustrated by the following figure.

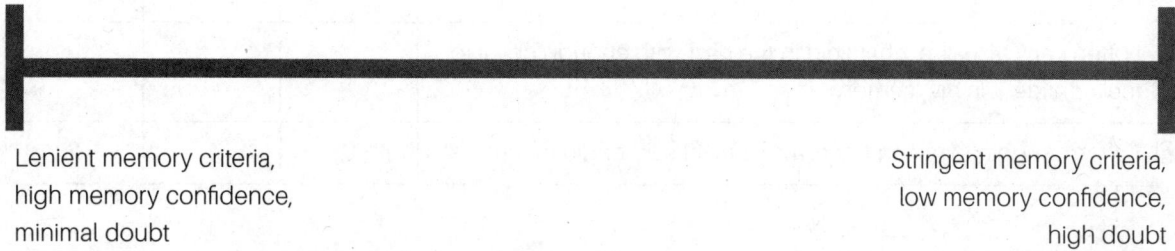

Lenient memory criteria,	Stringent memory criteria,
high memory confidence,	low memory confidence,
minimal doubt	high doubt

The key to understanding doubt about your past actions and decisions is determining whether you're demanding of yourself a perfect memory. If so, you'll have low memory confidence and will be burdened with excessive doubt. Use the next exercise to determine where you lie on the memory confidence continuum.

EXERCISE: Memory Confidence Measure

For the following list of statements about memory confidence, circle the number that reflects the extent to which each statement represents how you view your memory abilities.

Memory Confidence Statements	Not at All Like Me	A Little Like Me	A Lot Like Me
I have little confidence in my memory of past experiences.	0	1	2
I believe I have a poor memory.	0	1	2
People often remember more about the past than I do.	0	1	2
I have serious doubts that I recall the past accurately.	0	1	2
I am often mistaken in how I remember the past.	0	1	2
There are significant gaps in my memories of each day.	0	1	2

Memory Confidence Statements	Not at All Like Me	A Little Like Me	A Lot Like Me
I often forget and have to be reminded about tasks and errands that I'm expected to accomplish.	0	1	2
I often worry that something bad could happen because of my poor memory.	0	1	2
I often can't visualize what I did in the past with enough detail to feel confident in my memory.	0	1	2
I often struggle to remember exactly what I said or did in the past.	0	1	2

If you circled *a lot like me* for five or more statements, you may have low confidence in your memory. This would place you toward the low end of the continuum for memory confidence. If you're also a perfectionist, your standards of recall may be so high that you frequently experience doubts about your memory.

Charlotte frequently worked on confidential documents, so it was important that she secured her computer before leaving for the day. After leaving work she'd often think, *Did I close everything on my computer?* To relieve her doubt, she'd try to form an accurate memory of closing every application. But she often struggled to get a clear picture in her mind because the whole process of securing her computer had become so automatic. On a couple of occasions, the doubt was so intense that Charlotte went back to work to check her computer. Charlotte's perfectionism drove her to have unrealistic criteria for memory confidence.

Wrap-Up

Perfectionism is an important cause of doubt for many people. Having unrealistically high standards of performance for your actions, judgments, and decisions will cause you to have considerable self-doubt regarding your value and abilities. Remember, too, that unhealthy perfectionism leads to an important outcome that striving for excellence does not: perfectionism causes repeated experiences of failure that in turn strengthen self-doubt.

At the same time, low memory confidence will cause you to doubt the correctness of past actions and decisions. The culprit in this process is having unrealistic expectations for the accuracy of your memories. All memory is reconstructive, so we can never remember the past with 100 percent accuracy. If you demand this of yourself, then you're more likely to doubt your past actions and decisions. Once again perfectionism fuels excessive doubt.

There is one final construct we'll need to consider to understand excessive doubt: *risk aversion*, which is the central problem in anxiety. If risk aversion is associated with perfectionism, it can feel especially intolerable, and both of these processes will be potent accelerants for doubt.

CHAPTER 5

I Can't Take the Risk

Life is full of risk. We evaluate situations, circumstances, and experiences for the potential threat they pose to our physical or psychological well-being. And when we face the novel, ambiguous, or unknown, how we evaluate threat is especially relevant to how we respond. Since the possibility of threat can't be eliminated from most of life's problems and challenges, the critical question you face is *How much threat can you tolerate?* Some people have low risk tolerance, meaning if there's a small chance of harm, they avoid that situation. Other people have high risk tolerance. We might call these people daredevils or risk-takers because they're willing to engage in activities that have a high probability of causing harm. If you have low tolerance for risk, you'll experience more doubt than the high risk-takers.

No doubt finances come to mind when you think about risk. Financial advisors talk a lot about risk tolerance. They want to know how well you can tolerate the potential for loss in your savings and investments. We all have a natural aversion to losing money, but if your risk tolerance is low, you might say to your advisor, "I'd be far too worried about losses if my money was invested in something risky, so put me into something with a guaranteed return, something that is perfectly safe." If your risk tolerance is high you might say, "I want to get the highest possible return on my money. I can stand lots of volatility and won't worry if I go through a period of losses." Can you see how doubt plays a role in the low-risk person's approach to finances? Their worry is fueled by doubt and uncertainty about the future performance of their investments.

Risk tolerance is relevant in many aspects of living. Driving is a great example. Some drivers recklessly weave among cars on a busy highway, whereas the overly cautious, risk-averse person drives well under the speed limit in the slow lane. There are the thrill-seekers who love dangerous sports versus those who avoid speed, heights, or the unexpected. Risk tolerance can even play a role in our health. Some people take great risks by engaging in unhealthy habits while others are preoccupied with minimizing their health risks. The fact is that risk tolerance is a personality factor that affects how we live and relate to others. And risk tolerance is a significant contributor to excessive or problematic doubt.

> Low risk tolerance can increase the number of occasions when you feel threatened, which in turn will increase feelings of uncertainty and doubt about your sense of safety and well-being.

This chapter focuses on risk tolerance. We'll begin by diving into the topics of risk, risk tolerance, and our relationship with threat estimation. Catastrophic thinking diminishes risk tolerance, so it's an important factor to consider for understanding your sensitivity to risk. Assessment tools will help you to determine your level of risk tolerance and whether you catastrophize. And you'll reflect on how much value you place on safety, which is another factor in one's risk tolerance. But before we begin our discussion of risk, consider Derek's struggle with doubt in the context of his low risk tolerance.

Derek's Story: *Playing It Safe*

Derek was preoccupied with weighing the costs. He carefully considered the consequences of all his actions, decisions, and judgments, no matter their significance. He had difficulty thinking about the benefits of any course of action. Instead he focused on minimizing risk, avoiding to the best of his ability any possibility of a negative consequence that he'd later regret. Derek's motto was *Maximize safety and minimize threat*. This play-it-safe approach was driven by his aversion to risk—that is, his desire for maximum, even complete, certainty and predictability in life experiences. He believed that a greater sense of certainty and predictability reduced the likelihood of a negative outcome (threat) and the discomfort of persistent doubt. Playing it safe and taking as few chances as possible strengthened his conviction that he was making the right choice. In this way low risk tolerance led to *doing nothing*, which eliminated the discomfort of doubt.

Derek's cautious approach to life was evident in how he approached several of life's dilemmas. For example, he'd been renting a one-bedroom apartment for ten years, which had many downsides, including escalating rent, noisy neighbors, and a cramped space. Because of his good salary and secure job, he wondered if it was time to jump into the housing market before prices became untenable. Derek had excellent credit so he could easily qualify for a mortgage, but his risk aversion prevented him from making a move. He thought of various dangers associated with buying a house: *What if I become financially strapped? What if the house needs costly repairs? What if the operating costs of a house are more than I anticipated?* All these possible threats overwhelmed Derek, and so he decided that buying a house was too risky. Better to stick with his rental, the costs of which were well-known to him, than risk the uncertainty and unpredictability involved with home ownership. Of course, this decision had one huge downside for Derek: he was missing out on the chance to build equity through home ownership.

Derek's love life was another problem area. He dated occasionally but became overwhelmed with anxiety and uncertainty when he sensed a relationship was getting serious. When he felt this way, he would terminate the relationship. This fear of commitment was driven by his incessant doubts about whether the person he was dating was the right person for him, and the doubts were caused by Derek's risk-intolerant way of thinking: *What if I'm getting involved with a person who's too needy and demanding? Will I lose my freedom and control over my life? What if I commit and later regret it?* As you can see, all Derek could think about were the downsides, or risks, of continuing a relationship. And so he invariably ended the relationships before the commitment got too deep.

Derek's low risk tolerance influenced many of his actions and decisions throughout the day. He rarely expressed his opinion with friends or family for fear that doing so would lead to a confrontation. He stuck to what was routine and familiar because trying a new approach or doing something new always felt risky. He felt best when he was alone in the safety and security of his office and apartment. Derek preferred the predictability of his weekday routines and felt a little lost on the weekends when he wasn't following them. But, of course, life is full of surprises, even for the person with low risk tolerance. So Derek was often thrown into uncertainty, doubt, and anxiety related to actions he was forced to take and decisions he was forced to make when faced with a possible threat.

Knowing Risk

Simply stated, *risk* is the possibility that you will experience loss or injury. You can't think about risk without invoking ideas of threat, harm, danger, loss, or peril. We feel safe and secure when we're in situations devoid of risk. But total, absolute safety is impossible since being alive itself requires facing the risk of death. Many people are acutely aware of this fundamental reality of life. Living under a constant fear of death,

Risk is the perception of possible harm, threat, danger, or other negative consequences. Assessing the risks associated with our actions and decisions is a normal and necessary aspect of daily living.

they are fully aware that risk is inherent in life. If breathing itself (or more accurately the threat of not breathing) can feel risky for you at times, it is easy to see how you might meet every situation, action, and decision with an acute awareness of risk.

Risk aversion is a generalized tendency to view any uncertain outcome as undesirable and something to be avoided. Because uncertainty is a central ingredient in risk aversion, the risk-averse person will interpret doubt as indicating that the risk associated with a particular situation is unacceptable. The following figure presents risk aversion (or let's use the more inclusive term "risk tolerance") as an old-fashioned analog dial.

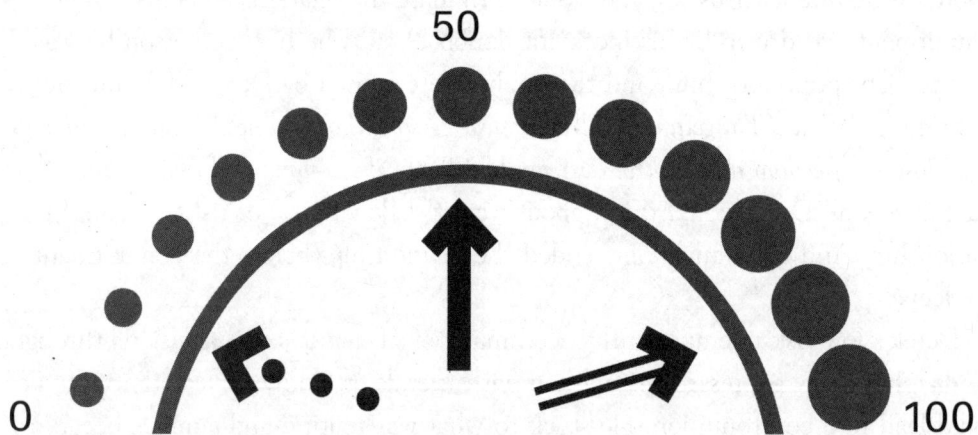

The dotted arrow represents a person with low risk tolerance. This person avoids practically everything associated with some risk because it makes them uncomfortable. But the person with very high risk tolerance, represented by the double-line arrow, might accept too much risk. This person is a risk-taker, and as such they are exposed to more negative consequences. No doubt the optimal is somewhere in the middle, which is represented by the solid arrow. This person has a healthy view of risk and is able to consider both the rewards and costs of an action or decision. Doubt experienced at this level of risk tolerance would beneficially help a person think through their options.

To understand the effects of risk tolerance on daily living, consider how it might affect your financial decision-making style. Imagine you have $100,000 in savings—a significant amount of money you have accumulated over the years for retirement—and are presented with two invest-ment opportunities. You can take the $100,000 and buy a certificate of deposit. It pays 4.5 percent annually, so in five years your deposit will have grown to $124,618. This amount is guaranteed and there is no risk of losing your investment. The second, much riskier option, is to invest the $100,000 in an AI start-up. The rate of return could be up to 12 percent annually, so in five years you might have $176,234 or much more—but you could also lose a good chunk of your initial investment if the stock does poorly. And of course there's no way to know for sure whether you'll win or lose on this stock. So, which option do you choose? Can you tolerate the risk of the AI stock or do you prefer the safety of the certificate of deposit? What you choose depends on your risk tolerance.

Maybe the answer to our hypothetical investment example is a little too obvious for you. You'd choose the certificate of deposit. But does that mean you're risk averse? To better understand where you sit on the risk tolerance dial, complete the next exercise.

EXERCISE: Risk Tolerance Measure

For the following statements about attitudes and perspectives on risk, place a checkmark to indicate the extent to which the statement applies to you.

Statement	Not Like Me	A Little Like Me	A Lot Like Me
I feel uncomfortable taking chances.			
I need to know how things will turn out when deciding which action to take.			
I try to avoid situations with uncertain outcomes.			
Deciding something on the spur of the moment fills me with dread.			
I'm terrible at improvising or thinking on my feet.			
I struggle to accept any losses, especially financial ones.			
I often think about how I can avoid losses or mishaps in my life.			
I worry that something bad is about to happen.			
I would choose to receive $100 now instead of taking a chance on a coin toss: $300 for heads or $0 for tails.			
I prefer to play it safe and not take chances.			

If you answered *a lot like me* for five or more statements, you likely have low tolerance for risk. As a person with a low tolerance for risk, you're more likely to interpret doubt as an indication that a situation is too risky. You would choose to avoid the situation. Of course, you might be risking a poor outcome in that process. Consider Derek's relationships. As soon as he felt doubt, he took it as a sign that continuing a relationship was too risky, and he quickly broke it off, preferring the safety of his single life. But the result was that he wasn't experiencing the satisfaction of a long-standing, fully committed relationship.

> Low tolerance for risk increases the likelihood that doubt will be misinterpreted as a sign of impending unbearable harm or a negative outcome.

Imagining the Worst

Do you find it easier to think of the negative than the positive in a situation? When making a decision, do you easily think about the costs associated with a choice but struggle to think of the benefits? Remember when Derek was considering buying a house? He focused only on the risks, weighing those much more heavily than the benefits.

A bias for catastrophic thinking will make you less risk tolerant. Consider gambling. The risk-averse person would never gamble because they easily see the prospect of loss. But the gambler doesn't focus on losing everything; instead, they think, *I have a good feeling about this bet; luck is on my side.* So, thinking the worst can be helpful for some decisions in life, such as whether to gamble, but unhealthy in others, such as whether to buy a house or continue dating in Derek's case. The fact is if you only think about significant threats or potential harm, then you will be risk averse. And thinking the worst is not balanced thinking. When people think the worst, they are overly focused on the negatives, the possibility of harm, and are not considering the potential benefits.

> Catastrophic thinking will make risk seem intolerable, something to avoid if at all possible.

Are you wondering if you are prone to catastrophic thinking? The next exercise will help you decide if you tend to assume the worst.

EXERCISE: The Catastrophic Perspective

For the statements below about how people experience perceived threat, harm, and danger, circle the number that best represents how well each statement describes you.

Statement	Does Not Describe Me	Somewhat Describes Me	Very Much Describes Me
The possibility of bad outcomes feels more likely than better outcomes.	0	1	2
Once I start thinking about a worst-case outcome, it's hard to consider any other possibility.	0	1	2
If I have doubts, my mind automatically goes to the worst possible outcome.	0	1	2
I can't stop myself from thinking the worst.	0	1	2
I'm more of a pessimist than an optimist.	0	1	2
When confronted with a problem or decision, the possibility of negative consequences comes to mind more easily than possibility of positive consequences.	0	1	2
People who know me best say that I have a tendency to catastrophize.	0	1	2
I often feel anxious.	0	1	2
I worry more than I should.	0	1	2
I get quite upset thinking about all the bad things that can happen to me or my loved ones.	0	1	2

If you agreed (circled 1 or 2) with five or more statements, you may have a tendency to overcatastrophize when making decisions. You find it easier to think of the potential downsides of your actions and decisions, and struggle to consider other, less dire options. And once you start imagining the worst, it's hard to let go of thinking about the worst possible outcome. This way of thinking is a major cause of anxiety and worry. The worst-case scenario will seem the most plausible, and so the risk becomes too great. Doubt confirms your feeling that the risk is too great, and so you avoid or procrastinate, even if it means missing out on a good opportunity. Next, we'll look at another process that contributes to risk intolerance: the search for safety.

Seeking Comfort

Although Derek felt dissatisfied with his life situation—doing a job that he knew well, living in the same apartment for ten years, and being a single person who could live life as he chose—there was something comforting to it. He definitely had a *comfort zone*, and within this zone, with doubt and risk held in check, he felt peace and calm. Whenever he started to feel anxious, Derek knew the best remedy was to get back to his comfort zone. The high value Derek placed on comfort contributed to his risk intolerance.

Psychologists define *safety seeking* as any behavioral or cognitive strategy used to diminish, avoid, or prevent the experience of anxiety, thereby achieving a sense of relief or comfort (Salkovskis 1991). They consider it a critical factor in the persistence of anxiety. If you run for safety at the first sign of anxiety, then you'll never learn that the anxiety-provoking situation isn't as dangerous as you think and that you're better equipped to cope with it than you realize.

> An overreliance on safety seeking will reduce your risk tolerance by contributing to a greater sensitivity to anxiety triggers.

You can probably see how safety seeking might contribute to risk intolerance. Imagine you are nervous about meeting new people. Your preferred safety-seeking behavior is to avoid meeting new people. But if you can't avoid a social situation that involves lots of people you don't know, you might stick very close to a friend you know well, or you might drink more alcohol than is usual so you feel less inhibited. These are all safety-seeking behaviors people use to deal with anxiety. They also have the unintended consequence of making you more risk intolerant of novel social situations.

There's evidence that safety seeking can undermine the effectiveness of CBT for treating anxiety. But it's worth noting that psychologists have challenged this view, arguing that some forms of safety seeking can be helpful (Rachman et al. 2008). Rachman and his colleagues listed seven conditions in which safety seeking can be adaptive. While it's my position in this book that safety seeking can diminish your tolerance of risk, I modified the statements in the following exercise to reflect their work.

EXERCISE: The Consequences of Safety Seeking

For the following statements about the effects of safety seeking, place a checkmark to indicate whether or not it applies to your experience of seeking safety when you're feeling anxious, distressed, or excessively doubtful.

Effects of Safety Seeking	Applies to Me	Does Not Apply to Me
I feel more confident and open to change when in my comfort zone.		
I feel more in control when I feel safe.		
I am more likely to accept corrective information when I feel safe.		
My anxiety and distress are quickly reduced when I escape to my comfort zone.		
I'm better able to question my thoughts and beliefs when I feel safe.		
I very much like the experience of relief when I escape to my comfort zone.		
Safety seeking plays an important role for me in maintaining emotional balance in my life.		

If you checked *applies to me* for most of the statements, then you likely believe that seeking safety is beneficial to coping with anxiety and distress. This means you're more likely to engage in safety seeking even if it might be detrimental in the long run. This way of coping could reduce your tolerance for risk. As you become more risk intolerant, you increasingly misinterpret doubt as a warning that some potential harm or negative consequence is in store for you. This causes you to avoid situations that make you feel doubt, which feeds anxiety and makes it a more difficult problem in your life.

Wrap-Up

Does risk excite you or scare you? Based on the assessment tools you completed in this chapter, what's your level of risk tolerance? If risk causes you considerable anxiety and worry, you likely try to reduce it as much as possible. You misinterpret every sign of doubt about some potential action or decision as indicating unacceptable risk, and so you avoid or at least procrastinate. But by engaging in such patterns, the risk-averse person becomes even more sensitive to doubt because they think it is an important early warning of unacceptable risk. For this reason, the person with low risk tolerance probably experiences more excessive doubt than the person who is more tolerant of risk.

A tendency to focus on worst-case outcomes, or catastrophizing, and a bias for placing a high premium on safety will reduce your tolerance for risk because you will consider any possibility of harm or discomfort unacceptable. Derek shied away from making important life decisions because all he could foresee were bad outcomes. He felt comfort with his present life circumstance, so why risk change? He lived by the phrase, "Better the devil you know than the devil you don't." Are you more like Derek than not? Are most of your actions and decisions dominated by efforts to minimize risk? If so, risk intolerance may be an important contributor to your anxiety, worry, and excessive doubt.

So far we've focused on *how* we doubt—that is, the various processes that can make doubt feel distressing. But *what* we doubt can have an equally negative influence on our mental health. In the next three chapters, we'll consider three types of doubt that can become problems: obsessive doubt involves a focus on past actions and decisions, relationship doubt is the fear of commitment, and religious doubt involves our relationship with God or our spirituality. We can doubt almost anything, but these three types of doubt illustrate the distinct ways that doubt can influence our life.

PART 2

The Many Faces of Doubt

CHAPTER 6

Obsessive Doubt

Imagine you're having a sleepless night. Your body is ready for sleep but your mind won't cooperate. It's flooded with all kinds of doubts, from the most mundane to more serious matters. It starts with *Did I lock all the windows and doors?* Of course you did, but you're not certain. The doubt intensifies and won't be pacified, and so you finally get up and check. Yes, they're all shut and locked. You go back to bed but within a few minutes the doubt returns: *Did I thoroughly check every window?* Eventually you're up checking the windows again. You go back to bed and doubt floods your mind about numerous issues: *Did I reset the alarm correctly? Should I check my phone in case I have an important message? Did I pay the credit card balance on time? What exactly did my doctor say about that mole on my back?* Have you had times like this, when you felt overwhelmed with doubt about almost everything? This is often the experience of those who struggle with obsessive doubt.

Relentless, obsessive doubt is the hallmark of OCD. The person with obsessive doubt has nagging uncertainty about the actions and decisions of everyday living, activities that most people do without a second thought. They seek a level of certainty, or conviction, that is impossible to attain. They especially fixate on the daily, repetitive actions that are habits. When we take a shower or brush our teeth, often our attention is focused on more important issues. Who stops to ponder whether they're thoroughly clean from the shower or that they've adequately brushed every tooth? Only people with obsessive doubt entertain such concerns.

> Frequent, unrelenting, and distressing doubt about the mundane actions and decisions of everyday living is the hallmark of obsessive doubt.

Obsessive doubt is the most mysterious of all the doubts we'll consider. It seems so irrational, even nonsensical, to others, and often the person struggling with it feels this way as well. For example, why get so upset by a doubt like *Did I change lanes too abruptly and almost cause an accident?* You didn't cause an accident, and maybe you made a mistake, so just forget about it. In this chapter we'll consider three pathways that lead to obsessive doubt and make doubt something you can't forget. The first is *inferential confusion*, which is mistakenly treating the possible as if it is the most probable. The second is low memory confidence, which we already discussed in chapter 4. And the third is excessive checking, repeating, and redoing, a form of coping with doubt that unintentionally magnifies its effects. But before we delve further into the problem of obsessive doubt, consider Kali's experience.

Kali's Story: *Drowning in Doubt*

Kali was overwhelmed by doubt more days than not. The smallest action or decision could trigger a new round of intense and distressing doubt. Some of these doubts made perfect sense, such as those that plagued her decision about whether to continue with her education or enter the workforce and start paying down her mounting student loan debt. A decision like this has far-reaching consequences, so who wouldn't have doubts about it? But Kali's doubt went well beyond major life decisions. It crept into everyday actions and decisions.

When leaving a room, for instance, she often doubted whether she flipped the light switch completely off even though she could turn around and see that the lights were off. She'd think, *What if I only turned the light switch partly off and there's still electricity getting to the light fixture? Could this start a fire?* Whenever she received a phishing email, she quickly deleted it but then had doubts about whether she'd opened the link by mistake. *What if my computer is infected with malware?* Even worse, *What if the email of everyone in my contact list is now infected with malware because of my careless action?* Casual conversations with friends or coworkers could elicit distressing doubts. Afterward, Kali would rehash what she'd said over and over in her mind, trying to decide whether she'd said something offensive or had betrayed a friend's confidence.

Kali knew most of her doubts were irrational. But they felt so distressing because she couldn't help but think about the possibility of terrible consequences. Who wouldn't feel terrible if they were responsible for causing others harm or injury? No one is perfect, and we all make mistakes and act without thinking through every action and decision.

But Kali felt she wouldn't be able to live with herself if she caused something bad to happen to others, even strangers. So the natural solution to the doubt was to check. But this terrible habit of rechecking, repeating, and reassurance seeking became her modus operandi and took over her life. These behaviors were so frequent and persistent they threatened her relationships and undermined her ability to function.

Does Kali's doubt sound familiar? Are you, too, caught in obsessive doubt? Or, you may be wondering how doubt could be so extreme that one would question every action and decision, even the most mundane activities of daily living. Kali's obsessive doubt didn't develop overnight, nor was it the result of some trauma in her life. Rather, it emerged gradually over time, starting in her early teens. As she continued to consider possible harm to herself or to others as *probable* harm, she became more and more intolerant of the uncertainty. She lost confidence in her memory of past actions and decisions, and relied increasingly on the three Rs of obsessive doubt: rechecking, repeating, and reassurance.

Identifying Obsessive Doubt

We all have doubts pop into our mind that are pretty irrational when we stop to think about them. For instance, *Did I accidentally offend my friend, and now she's upset with me? What if my boss can tell I don't respect him? Did I humiliate myself at the office party?* These are doubts about common activities, and you may be wondering if they are normal or representative of obsessive doubt.

> Everyone experiences flashes of doubt from time to time that may seem obsessive. How you respond to this momentary doubt determines whether it becomes obsessive.

The next exercise gives you an opportunity to assess your doubting experiences. It consists of fifteen statements based on themes commonly found in measures of OCD.

EXERCISE: Obsessive Doubt Scale

Read the following statements and circle the number that best represents how much each statement applies to (or describes) your experience of doubt.

Statements	Never Applies	Occasionally Applies	Often Applies	Always Applies
I often wonder if I performed the ordinary activities of daily living correctly or completely.	0	1	2	3
I tend to worry that my actions or decisions have accidentally caused others harm.	0	1	2	3
I have a fear of making mistakes in what I say or do.	0	1	2	3
I often feel a strong urge to check, repeat, or redo prior actions.	0	1	2	3
I can be more convinced by what might happen than by what I actually see or hear.	0	1	2	3
I can imagine a catastrophe happening even in the ordinary activities of daily living.	0	1	2	3
I often check and recheck things such as faucets, light switches, the stove, doors, windows, and the like.	0	1	2	3
Thinking that something dangerous might happen can be just as troubling as dealing with something that is actually dangerous.	0	1	2	3
I often try to recall as much detail as possible about a past action or decision to reassure myself that I've caused no harm.	0	1	2	3
The harder I try to remember something I said or did, the less I seem to remember.	0	1	2	3
Repeated checking causes me considerable distress and interferes with my life.	0	1	2	3
I have a vivid imagination, especially regarding potential harm or danger.	0	1	2	3
Just thinking about the possibility of harm or danger is all the evidence I need to take action.	0	1	2	3
I waste a lot of time because I check over and over.	0	1	2	3

Statements	Never Applies	Occasionally Applies	Often Applies	Always Applies
Even the possibility that what I said or did could cause harm is enough for me to take precautions.	0	1	2	3

If you circled 2 or 3 for many of the items on the Obsessive Doubt Scale, then consider whether you experience obsessive doubt. (This scale and many other worksheets are available for download at the website for this book, http://www.newharbinger.com/55756.) Kali realized she had a serious problem with compulsive checking. Not only did she score all the checking statements highly, but much of her behavior was driven by a strong fear of causing harm to others or of making mistakes that would lead to dire consequences. Kali's life was no more accident prone than the rest of us, so her obsessive doubts were driven not by reality but by confusing the possibility of harm with the probability of harm.

Before we delve into the topic of inferential confusion as a root cause of obsessive doubt, a brief caveat is in order. If you had a high score on the Obsessive Doubt Scale, consider seeking a consultation with a certified mental health professional to determine if you meet the diagnostic criteria for OCD. Because doubt is a central feature of OCD, you'll find this chapter highly relevant (and the later interventions useful), but there are highly effective, specific treatments for OCD that will take you much further in your recovery. You can think of our current focus on doubt as a supplement that you can use in conjunction with a more effective and targeted course of CBT for OCD (for further discussion see Clark 2019).

Possible but Not Probable

How many times have you backed out of your driveway or some other parking space and driven off without giving it a second thought? What if a momentary doubt flashed through your mind and you thought, *Did I back over someone?* You might then think, *Obviously I didn't because I didn't see anyone, I didn't hear any screams, and I didn't feel a bump from hitting someone.* Your conclusion: *What a silly thought; of course I didn't back over anyone.*

If you don't experience obsessive doubt, you might think this is an absurd example. But what makes it absurd is your ability to use sensory information (sight and sound) to correct your thinking. You focus not on what is possible (tragically, drivers do back over pedestrians sometimes) but on what is probable. There's an infinitesimally small possibility that you accidentally backed over someone and drove away without knowing, and you dismiss it. And so the momentary doubt, the question, disappears quickly, in the blink of an eye.

But this is not Kali's experience when such a doubt flashes through her mind. Instead, she immediately feels a pit in her stomach, her body tenses, her heart pounds, and she feels breathless. Instantly she imagines a person bleeding and severely injured, stumbling, crying for help. The anxiety and uncertainty build, with Kali feeling a strong compulsion to go back and check. She knows this thought process is absurd, but she must check to relieve her troubled mind. So Kali goes back and checks the parking space for evidence that she didn't harm someone, but one check is never enough. She gets caught in a protracted cycle of repeated checking that leaves her frustrated, upset, and late for work. Kali's experience is an example of obsessive doubt rooted in the process of *inferential confusion*, in which she treats a possibility as if it is probable. It goes like this:

Is it possible that I accidentally backed over a person? I don't recall looking carefully in the rearview mirror before starting to back out. I may have been a little too quick backing out because I was in a hurry. My mind was not on my driving; I was thinking about what I face at work today. I've read horrifying accounts of people accidentally backing over children, so I know this happens. Is it not entirely possible that I could've driven off and not noticed someone lying on the ground? Maybe I knocked them unconscious so they couldn't yell. Maybe there was an eyewitness who took down my license number. They'll report me to the police and I'll be charged with a hit-and-run. I'd be forever traumatized by committing such a reckless and cruel act toward an innocent person. I better go back and check to make sure no one is injured.

In this example you can see that Kali is treating the possibility of backing over a person as though it were also probable, not just an infinitesimally small possibility. Psychologists O'Connor and Aardema (2012) note there are two core processes in inferential confusion: a distrust of your senses, including common sense, and an overinvestment in remote possibilities. You can see this in Kali's faulty reasoning about backing over a pedestrian. She doesn't trust what she saw and heard (no victim) or the commonsense reality that drivers don't have a habit of driving over people without knowing it. She becomes fixated on the ever-so-remote possibility of accidentally hitting a pedestrian, and all her obsessive doubt and checking follow from that.

> When common sense is abandoned in favor of fixating on remote possibilities, obsessive doubt will prevail.

Anyone can fall prey to inferential confusion from time to time. Your toddler has a fever, and you need to give him a prescribed medication. You carefully measure out the right dosage but then find yourself checking and rechecking to make sure you measured correctly. You're a conscientious and cautious parent, but in this instance you don't trust yourself and instead act on the remote possibility that you made a mistake. But when is a little inferential confusion too much? Complete the next exercise to determine whether or not you easily fall into inferential confusion when dealing with common activities of daily living.

EXERCISE: Inferential Confusion Bias

Below are six scenarios that involve doubt about some action or decision. In each case you could respond to the doubt with common sense or with inferential confusion. The commonsense view focuses on the most likely outcome, whereas inferential confusion involves a distrust of your senses and a focus on remote possibilities. Compose a commonsense and inferential confusion perspective for each scenario. Kali's response to the first scenario is provided as an example.

Doubting Scenario	Commonsense Perspective	Inferential Confusion Perspective
Could I have poisoned my guests by cross-contaminating vegetables when cooking raw chicken?	• I have never poisoned anyone with my cooking. • I'm always careful when handling raw chicken. • I obsessively follow the hygiene rules for handling raw chicken. • Given the huge quantities of chicken consumed, the incidence of illness is remarkably low.	• I know vulnerable people can get fatally ill from salmonella and campylobacter poisoning due to cross-contamination with raw chicken. • Although I'm careful, it is possible to make mistakes. • I'd feel extreme guilt and shame if someone got sick from my cooking. • I couldn't live with myself knowing I was careless and caused harm to others. • I can't remember doing a thorough clean after cutting up the chicken.

Doubting Scenario	Commonsense Perspective	Inferential Confusion Perspective
Was I completely honest when talking to a coworker about an important work issue?		
At work wondering if I left a pot on a hot burner at home?		
Drive past a cyclist and have an intrusive doubt that maybe I drove too close to her.		

Doubting Scenario	Commonsense Perspective	Inferential Confusion Perspective
Notice that the car is making an unusual noise and wonder if it'll break down on a busy highway.		
Did I offend my sister-in-law when I gave my opinion about a family problem?		

Which column did you find most difficult to complete? Which response was most believable, common sense or inferential confusion? If you encountered these doubting scenarios, could you use common sense to quell your doubt, or would you fall into inferential confusion? Kali experienced obsessive doubt because she only focused on the possibility of fatally poisoning her guests rather than truly consider the common-sense perspective. Because she couldn't remember every detail about cleaning the utensils and counter surfaces after cutting up the raw chicken, she doubted her commonsense thinking even more. It is this way of thinking that can turn momentary doubt into obsessive doubt.

Low Memory Confidence

Chapter 4 on perfectionism introduced you to the problem of low memory confidence. You'll recall that low memory confidence is a feeling of uncertainty about whether you have an accurate and detailed recollection of a prior action or decision. *I can't recall hearing the dead bolt latch when I locked the door. I can't remember everything I said to my neighbor when we had that long conversation yesterday. I can't remember whether I attached the ground wire when changing the light fixture.* If you're a perfectionist, your standards for recall may be so high that you have little confidence in your memory. But you don't have to be a perfectionist to have low memory confidence. Any time you question your memory about a past action or decision, you open the door to obsessive doubt.

> When in doubt we automatically try to recall the details of a past action to reassure ourselves that a dreaded outcome will not happen. If memory confidence is low, reassurance is unattainable and obsessive doubt persists.

If you are wondering if low memory confidence is contributing to your obsessive doubt, review your responses to the Memory Confidence Measure in chapter 4. It will be difficult to use common sense to counter obsessive doubt if you have little confidence in what you remember about past actions or decisions. For example, Kali believed she had a poor memory and so was unable to reassure herself that past actions or decisions were correct or complete. She could not let go of the past because even a remote possibility of a bad outcome was unacceptable. To overcome her obsessive doubt, Kali needed to realize that her memories of most of the routine activities of daily living were sufficiently accurate to live normally.

Obsessive doubt is usually associated with the common activities of daily living. But do we really need an accurate and detailed memory of all the little things we do day in and day out? This next exercise asks you to rate how well you remember doing a variety of routine activities.

EXERCISE: Memory for Daily Activities

The following is a sample of routine activities. Next to each activity place a checkmark in the column that best represents how much you *consciously* remember doing that particular activity on any given day. For example, you're pretty confident you brushed your teeth this morning, but it's such a habit that you recall very little about it, so maybe you give it a 10% recall. On the other hand, you're a very cautious driver, so you have a much clearer recall of stopping at stop signs, so you give it an 80% recall.

Activities of Daily Living	10% Recall	25% Recall	50% Recall	80% Recall	100% Recall
Complete and thorough brushing of teeth					
Turning on signal light well before making a turn					
Coming to complete stop at every stop sign					
Thoroughly cleaning every part of your body when showering					
Checking expiration dates when grocery shopping					
Putting detergent in the dishwasher or washing machine					
Securely strapping child into car seat					
Fastening own seatbelt					

What did you notice? Odds are you had little recall of many of these habits of daily living. Does this surprise you? The fact is we don't need a complete, conscious memory of our routine activities. We just do them without a second thought. The seeds of obsessive doubt are sown when we demand a complete and detailed memory of past actions and decisions, including those above. When we demand this of ourselves, we're trying to take conscious, effortful control of habits that operate best via the automatic processes of our brain.

Rechecking, Repeating, and Redoing

We all check and maybe even recheck past actions and decisions. If the task is important or has significant long-term consequences, we're more likely to check. Let's say you're sending an email to multiple recipients about a stance you're taking on a workplace issue. Management will receive the email as well as your coworkers. So, before clicking send, you reread the email, maybe several times, to make sure its tone and substance are diplomatic. If taken the wrong way, you could get yourself into real trouble. Or let's say you post something on social media that is unusual for you. You might review it several times, concerned that you could experience ridicule. Or say you're ready to leave on a vacation and you check several times to make sure you didn't forget your passport. These are examples of "normal" checking. But when does checking cross the line and become a problem that contributes to obsessive doubt?

People with an OCD diagnosis display all sorts of extreme checking behavior. A person repeatedly retraces his driving route, checking the ditches and surrounding area to make sure he didn't injure a pedestrian or cyclist. Another person has a fear of excrement and so inspects every aspect of the house over and over looking for brown specks. I had a client who repeatedly checked the freezer to make sure no one was locked inside. She realized it was an absurd idea but still couldn't resist the powerful urge to check. Others will spend hours checking and rechecking appliances, windows, doors, faucets, light switches, and so forth before going to bed or leaving the house or apartment. These may seem like obvious examples of problematic checking that lead to obsessive doubt but even less extreme checking can fuel obsessive doubt.

> Frequent checking, repeating, and redoing can paradoxically increase doubt even though the behavior is intended to ease doubts.

Are you wondering if your rechecking, repeating, and redoing habits are contributing to your problem with doubt? The next exercise lists nine characteristics of excessive checking. Take a moment to reflect on your experiences of checking and consider whether any of these characteristics are applicable to you.

EXERCISE: The Extreme Checking Checklist

Place a checkmark beside each characteristic that is relevant to your experience of checking how well you performed routine daily activities such as turning off appliances, switching off lights, locking doors and windows, conversing with others, posting messages, and the like.

- ☐ One or two checks is not enough.

- ☐ The urge to check is irresistible and feels uncontrollable.

- ☐ Its frequency significantly interferes with daily living.

- ☐ Frustration, annoyance, and even distress increase significantly with subsequent checks. (*Why can't I just stop. I want to stop checking.*)

- ☐ Your memory of past actions degrades with repeated checking.

☐   The check is narrowly focused on averting serious harm to self or others.

☐   Its purpose is to reduce a heightened sense of responsibility for causing or preventing harm to self or others.

☐   It's intended to reduce criticism or guilt for actions and decisions.

☐   There's a reliance on achieving a vague, subjective internal state of feeling like enough has been done to know when to stop checking.

Are any of these characteristics relevant to your checking and repeating experiences? The more boxes you checked, the more likely it is that repeated checking is contributing to your obsessive doubt. All nine characteristics undermine the effectiveness of checking so that one check is not enough. As you engage in successive checks, the uncertainty builds and the feeling of knowing that you completed the task correctly eludes your grasp. This may seem counterintuitive, but repeated checking negatively affects your memory. If you're repeatedly checking to assuage a fear about leaving your door unlocked, for instance, it'll be harder with each successive attempt to remember whether you did the check correctly and completely. Both your confidence in your memory of previous checks and your ability to focus on the sensory details of your check, in a way that might help you retain the memory, become degraded.

Wrap-Up

Waking up to a new day and the prospect of facing the routine activities of daily living can feel daunting to those with obsessive doubt. *Did I get out of bed correctly? Am I thoroughly clean from my shower? Did I wash and dry my breakfast dishes completely so they are free of dirt and germs? Did I trap the cat in one of the rooms by mistake? Did I unplug all the appliances before leaving the house?* Already at the beginning of the day, obsessive doubt feels unrelenting. It continues throughout the day, creating unbearable levels of anxiety, worry, and guilt; and it doesn't stop until you finally fall asleep.

As we have seen, obsessive doubt is driven by three processes: confusing probability with possibility, low memory confidence, and the toxic effects of repeated checking. Obsessive doubt is not the most common type of doubt, but when it strikes it has serious consequences. It can cause significant personal distress and make it practically impossible to meet the challenges of daily living. If you experience obsessive doubt, you'll find many of the interventions in the last three chapters effective antidotes. You'll learn how to use the commonsense perspective, strengthen memory confidence, and resist the urge to check. In the meantime, we'll turn to doubt that can undermine your ability to form a healthy intimate relationship.

CHAPTER 7

Relationship Doubt

What gives your life meaning and purpose? One of your first thoughts might be the quality of your relationships. Close connection to the most important people in our life, most notably our intimate partner, is critical to satisfying our deepest need for love, affirmation, and value. But excessive doubt can frustrate your ability to establish a healthy intimate relationship.

Having an intimate partner contributes greatly to happiness and life satisfaction. Being in a loving and accepting intimate relationship is associated with having a more positive view of yourself and finding greater meaning in life (Czyżowska et al. 2020). The importance of a loving, intimate relationship for one's well-being and mental health cannot be overstated. Anything that threatens the health of your intimate relationship, such as excessive doubt, must be addressed.

> Doubt can undermine the quality of your intimate relationship or perpetuate a fear of committing to a lifetime partner.

In this chapter you'll learn how excessive doubt creates commitment problems for people who are in intimate relationships or not. We'll start by exploring the nature of relationship doubt, and I'll provide assessment tools to help you determine whether unhealthy doubt is undermining your search for love and affirmation. We'll examine three core questions that define excessive relationship doubt. Not all doubt is bad for a relationship; there's a healthy form of doubt that you actually need when making important decisions about an intimate partner. The final section presents several key relationship questions that can guide you in making decisions about further commitment. But before we begin, consider Toby's story that illustrates how excessive doubt created a strong fear of commitment that stymied his efforts to form a deep and meaningful connection with an intimate partner.

Eric's Story: *A Crisis of Commitment*

Eric a single man in his mid-thirties, had a promising career with an IT start-up, financial security, a few close friends, and several interesting recreational activities. Despite all this good fortune, Eric felt miserable, alone, and depressed. He experienced an emptiness that he knew was caused by not having a loving intimate partner. He believed he'd failed in love and was now destined for a life of loneliness. Although he dated, nothing ever seemed to pan out. Eric knew he was part of the problem—he had a strong *fear of commitment*. As soon as a casual dating relationship showed signs of getting serious, Eric broke it off. His mistrust and lack of commitment were fueled by powerful doubts about getting too involved with a romantic partner.

There were several reasons for Eric's relationship insecurity. At the top of the list was a really painful breakup. He had fallen in love with a woman who had seemed like his perfect match. The relationship developed quickly, and they talked of moving in together. Eric's life was filled with new meaning and happiness, and he dreamt of their future together. But she suddenly ended the relationship. It took Eric many months to work through the emotional pain. Breakups are hard for everyone, but Eric struggled with low self-esteem and a profound fear of rejection, which made breakups especially challenging for him. As a result of this breakup, he resolved to never let himself be so vulnerable again. He would protect his freedom and independence rather than risk the emotional pain of another breakup.

Eric's fear of commitment affected every dating encounter. He tended to be aloof and never let a romantic partner get too close. If one asked serious questions about their future, placed high expectations and demands on his time, or wanted a deeper level of intimacy, he ended the relationship. While dating, he continually questioned the relationship, and this is where doubt played a pivotal role. He wondered things like:

Is she really attracted to me, or am I just a friend to her?

Maybe she's tired of me and looking for an excuse to break it off?

Do I really want this or am I better off by myself?

Am I starting to get my hopes up, which makes me more vulnerable?

Is she right for me, or could there be someone else I'm more compatible with?

Am I settling for less because I feel alone and depressed?

Eric couldn't find satisfactory answers to his questions. He considered doubt a sign that the relationship was not going well. Better to break it off before he got in too deep and felt devastated by the other person's rejection.

Relationship Doubts and Fear of Commitment

Doubt can have a negative impact on romantic love whether you're in a relationship or not. As we saw in Eric's story, relationship doubt can foment a fear of commitment and an avoidance of deep emotional connections. Doubt causes you to miss promising opportunities so that you remain in a state of involuntary singlehood. But for those in an intimate relationship, doubt can weaken their emotional connection with an intimate partner. Complete the next two exercises to determine whether relationship doubt is a problem for you.

> Misinterpreting doubt as a signal of imminent rejection will contribute to a fear of commitment and possibly an unwarranted breakup.

EXERCISE: Fear of Commitment Scale

The following statements represent attitudes, beliefs, and behaviors about relationship commitment. Circle the number that most closely corresponds to how well the statement describes you.

Statements	Not Like Me	Like Me	Very Much Like Me
I prefer short-term casual dating relationships to longer-term relationships.	0	1	2
I have difficulty trusting another person.	0	1	2
I am especially sensitive to rejection.	0	1	2
I'm emotionally distant and hesitate to talk about my feelings in a relationship.	0	1	2
I struggle with low self-esteem.	0	1	2
I guard myself against being emotionally vulnerable due to past breakups.	0	1	2

Statements	Not Like Me	Like Me	Very Much Like Me
I will break off a relationship if I sense my partner's interest is waning.	0	1	2
I feel uneasy when a partner starts talking about our future together.	0	1	2
I fear the emotional dependency of another and limits on my freedom.	0	1	2
I feel anxious when the person I'm dating progresses too quickly with intimacy and talk of love.	0	1	2
The thought of spending the rest of my life with one person scares me.	0	1	2
I'm frightened of hurting someone who is emotionally fragile and highly invested in a relationship.	0	1	2
I need to feel convinced that this person is right for me before I let myself become emotionally involved.	0	1	2
I feel uncomfortable with the expectations and responsibilities of an intimate relationship.	0	1	2
I'm highly sensitive to any negative or critical comments from the person I'm dating.	0	1	2
I'm always wondering if the person I'm dating is genuinely interested in or committed to me.	0	1	2
I often think back to the emotional hurt I experienced from past breakups.	0	1	2

Eric would score a 1 or 2 for many of these items. A score of 10 or more suggests you might have a problem with fear of commitment. Note that this scale is not a researched measure; it's intended as a guide to help you determine whether you have a commitment problem. Consider discussing your scale responses with a therapist or a close and trusted family member or friend. Find out if they agree with your self-evaluation. If you are currently in a relationship, you will find the next exercise even more relevant for gauging your level of relationship doubt.

EXERCISE: Relationship Doubt Scale

The statements below reflect various aspects of relationship doubt. Circle the number that most closely corresponds to how well each statement describes you.

Statements	Not Like Me	Like Me	Very Much Like Me
I often wonder if I really love my partner.	0	1	2
I question whether this relationship is right for me.	0	1	2
I often wonder if I'd be better off with someone else.	0	1	2
I'm not sure that my partner really loves me.	0	1	2
It's hard to dismiss, or move past, doubtful thoughts about the relationship.	0	1	2
I frequently ask my partner whether they love me.	0	1	2
I'm uncertain whether my partner is "the one"—my true soulmate.	0	1	2
I often feel our relationship is not right for me.	0	1	2
I try to convince myself that I love my partner, but I'm left with doubts.	0	1	2
I wonder if I'd be better off leaving this relationship.	0	1	2
I often look for evidence that our relationship is sound.	0	1	2
I'm frightened that my partner no longer loves me.	0	1	2
I need repeated reassurance that our relationship is healthy.	0	1	2
I feel quite anxious when I start questioning our relationship.	0	1	2
I wonder if my partner would be better off without me.	0	1	2
I'm not sure we're the best for each other.	0	1	2

If you scored 1 or 2 on eight or more statements, personal doubt may be contributing to the dissatisfaction and disconnection you're feeling in an intimate relationship. If you scored much higher—that is, 20 or more—I recommend that you consult a mental health professional to determine if your relationship doubt reflects underlying OCD.

> Look deeply within yourself if you're feeling miserable about your intimate-partner relationship or about being single. Excessive doubt may be the hindrance to greater fulfillment in your relationships.

Take a moment to consider the impact that excessive relationship doubt has in your personal life. In the space below, write about how doubt has affected your ability to establish or maintain a loving relationship. The example illustrates one way doubt can undermine an intimate-partner relationship.

It's hard to be intimate with my partner when I'm doubting. I tend to withdraw physically and say very little; I keep my thoughts and feelings to myself. She keeps asking what's wrong, but I refuse to tell her about my doubts; they will only cause tension and conflict. I keep thinking that I've settled for less than what's best for me, and this makes me short-tempered and annoyed with her. I have only regrets and it makes me angry; I feel like she tricked me into marriage. In all, I feel empty, sad, and angry because I'm missing out on a truly close, stable, and affirming relationship.

_____

_____

_____

_____

_____

_____

Now that you've determined whether you have unhealthy relationship doubt, it's time to delve into the problem more deeply. There are three key questions that drive relationship doubt.

What Is Love?

I'm sure you'll agree this is a loaded question. Love is a critical part of humanity, but how would you define it? Do you know for certain when it's present or absent in your intimate relationship? For an emotional experience so vital to the health of our relationships, we often have a surprisingly fuzzy understanding of love. Did you ever receive any instruction about love? You probably learned about sex, hopefully from a trusted source, but love and sex are very different and should never be confused.

Am I in love? Do I really love this person? Have I fallen out of love? are the types of questions you might ask yourself when you're doubting your love for another. When the doubt becomes extreme, it can undermine a healthy relationship and lead to an unwise decision. Excessive doubt about love is often caused by a misunderstanding of love. In our social-media-and-entertainment-saturated culture, it's easy to equate "love" with "passion" and "intimacy." While passion and intimacy are often factors in love, if the passion and sexual excitement—the chemistry—you once felt for your partner have dropped off dramatically, do you assume you've fallen out of love?

Ultimately, love is a deeply personal and multifaceted experience that depends on our biology, personality, upbringing, culture, life experiences, past relationships, and the like. It's easy to have doubts about love because of its subjective, intuitive nature. A way forward with your doubt begins with a more complete understanding of love. One of the best descriptions of love I've encountered was generated for me by Microsoft's Copilot:

> *A deeply personal [human] experience that includes emotional connection, commitment and support, passion and intimacy, mutual respect and understanding, selflessness and sacrifice, and growth and transformation.*

Notice that Copilot characterizes love in broad terms covering six facets of relational experience. These facets of love are highly subjective in their own right and hard to identify, but the definition warns against reducing love to a single dimension, such as passion or intimacy. Is it possible your doubts about love are rooted in a narrow, distorted definition of love? The next exercise gives you an opportunity to evaluate some of your ideas and beliefs about love.

> A fuller, more robust understanding of love is needed to overcome the ups and downs of a loving relationship.

EXERCISE: Beliefs About Romantic Love

Place a checkmark beside the following statements that are relevant to your beliefs about love.

☐   True love is spontaneous and happens quickly at the beginning of a relationship.

☐   True love is forever; it is continuous, never changing.

☐   When one is truly in love, there is excitement, a longing for your partner.

☐   When one is in love, intimacy and sex are always erotic and mutually satisfying.

☐   Couples in love rarely have arguments or disagreements.

☐   Genuine love overcomes all obstacles and difficulties in the relationship.

☐   When you're in love, there is a chemistry between you and your partner.

☐   There is only one person that can be my true love.

☐   If I'm in love, I'll be excited to make new discoveries about my partner.

☐   I can overlook any shortcomings in my partner if I'm truly in love.

☐   When one is in love, there are no secrets in the relationship.

☐   Genuine love means I'll be selfless, always putting my partner before myself.

☐   If I'm in love, I'll feel fulfilled and complete.

☐   If I'm truly in love, I'll always forgive my partner.

The preceding statements are not completely false, but taken to extremes they create unrealistic expectations for what it means to be in love. The more statements you checked as relevant, the greater the risk you'll experience unhealthy doubt about whether or not you're in love.

Eric was confused about his feelings. He questioned whether he was capable of love. He believed that true love was quick and spontaneous, there was only one person he could love, that sex should always be exciting and mutually satisfying, and that love could conquer all in a relationship. No wonder he continually doubted his feelings about others and—especially after the end of a relationship in which he felt rejected—concluded that he was doomed to be loveless. A deeper, multifaceted view of love is key to countering excessive doubt and ensuring a healthy relationship.

Am I Loved?

People often focus on whether their partner loves them. Maybe you have unrelenting doubt that is eating away at you. Does my partner really love me? Are they bored or frustrated with the relationship? Is there someone else?

Doubt about your partner's love can have a devastating effect on the relationship. It can cause you to misread cues and prematurely end the relationship. Even worse, it can lead to jealousy, anger, and even intimate-partner violence as you try to work out your uncertainties about your partner. (It is crucial to note that violence in relationships is never acceptable. If this is an issue for you, seek professional help without delay.) As with most questions related to love, these doubts are often rooted in a distorted, idealized view of intimate relationships. If you are single and have a fear of commitment, a biased, idealized view of love may cause you to conclude that a romantic relationship is too likely to cause rejection and emotional hurt for you to take a chance.

How do you know your partner loves you? It's impossible to read someone's mind. You can only infer they love you from what they say, how they behave toward you, the emotions they express, and possibly their body language. And how you interpret your partner's behavior is affected by your beliefs and expectations, making the whole process highly subjective. Have you ever thought deeply about what you are looking for in a relationship, and what you expect of a partner? This next exercise gives you a chance to do just that—to put your ideals and expectations under a microscope and evaluate whether they're contributing to upsetting doubts about your partner's love.

EXERCISE: An Idealized Account of a Partner's Love

In this exercise you're asked to describe what your partner would have to do to relieve all your doubts and instill confidence in you that they love you. If you've always been uncertain of your partner's love, you'll have to imagine what it would take to eliminate all doubt. Think outside the bounds of reality. Even if your ideas are extreme or totally unrealistic, if they're what you'd need to be certain of your partner's love, write them down. But first, read what Eric had to say.

I know that what I'm about to write is totally unrealistic, but this is what I think it would take to be totally certain of a partner's love. I'd need to believe that she is totally into me, that our relationship is the most important thing in her life, and that I always come first. She would need to have a strong physical attraction to me, be sexually responsive to all my advances, and often initiate sexual experiences. She'd need to tell me often how much she loves and adores me. She'd always find me interesting and funny; we'd totally enjoy each other's company. She'd keep reassuring me that she'd never leave me, that her life would be devastated without me. I'd know that she loves me by how she behaves around me. We'd always be in agreement and never argue or have a difference of opinion. Only then would I be convinced we are true soulmates and that she truly loves me.

Now it's your turn. Use a separate sheet of paper if you need more space.

_____

_____

_____

_____

_____

_____

_____

What do you think of your description? Is it realistic or even humanly possible? No doubt you can see unrealistic elements in Eric's description, but what about yours? If you agree that your expectations are unrealistic, then looking to your partner to erase your doubt is not the answer. Instead, work on adjusting your expectations of your partner, understanding the real parameters of emotional connection, and accepting there is no lifetime guarantee in human relations.

> Love is a gift. Given love's mysteries, it can only be accepted and mutually shared without guarantees or naïve assurances.

Is This Right for Me?

Do you think there is someone special for you just waiting to be discovered? Maybe you end one relationship after another because they don't feel right to you. Or you're currently in an intimate relationship but you have doubts. *Are we the best match for each other? Have I found my soulmate—the One?* These questions boil down to doubts about the rightness of the relationship. When Eric asked himself these questions, the answers caused him to doubt the rightness of the relationship, and so it ended in a breakup. He could never achieve the certainty he desired that the relationship was right for him.

Sheva Rajaee, author of *Relationship OCD*, calls this way of thinking the "Myth of the One" (MOTO). She describes it this way:

> *If only you could find the right one, the right person, all your pain and suffering will vanish, and you'll live happily ever after. You won't need to work too hard on your relationship,*

because it will feel natural and easy! You'll just know it when you feel it, and if you don't feel it, you're probably settling. (2022, 2)

It is very likely that your doubts about the rightness of a relationship are rooted in MOTO. But notice that Rajaee uses the word "myth," because there is no one-and-only-one person out there for you. This way of thinking leaves you stuck in excessive relationship doubt. You're likely to end up alone, like Eric, waiting for the person of your dreams to materialize. Or you may break off a healthy relationship because you're not certain your partner is "the One." The thought that you're settling for less is so troubling you end up making the wrong decision. The next exercise can help you determine if MOTO is fueling your doubts.

EXERCISE: Probing the Rightness of Your Relationship

Think about your most serious intimate relationship either past or current. What about that relationship made you feel it wasn't right for you, that your partner was not the One?

_____

_____

_____

1. What's the closest you've ever come to having the right relationship? What made it close to being right? How close was your partner to being the One?

_____

_____

2. What would make you feel like you found the One, that special person who is the best match for you? This is your MOTO.

_____

_____

_____

Do you think your MOTO is realistic? Are you seeking a "perfect" match when perfection doesn't exist? This was Eric's problem. Thinking he needed to have no doubts about a relationship, that he had to be convinced his partner was the one and only special person destined to be his soulmate, in part drove his fear of commitment. What he didn't realize was that he was on a quest with no end in sight.

> It's possible there is someone closer to your MOTO than your current partner since there are eight billion inhabitants on the planet.

The Necessity of Doubt

Should I initiate or respond to this dating invitation? Should I make a deeper commitment to my partner? Should I break off this relationship? These are some of life's most important questions with serious, long-term consequences. You want to think them through and make the best decision for you and your partner. So many people are caught in unhealthy, even toxic, intimate-partner relationships characterized by abuse, hypercriticalness, disrespect, selfishness, manipulation and control, mistrust and jealousy, an inability to communicate freely and honestly, incompatible interests, a lack of intimacy or emotional connection, and so on. An unhealthy relationship can have a profound impact on your mental health and well-being. So, you want to get it right—and a *healthy* dose of doubt can actually be helpful in that aim.

So far in this chapter we've been focused on excessive relationship doubt and how it can sabotage your efforts to find love or to do the hard work of building a healthy relationship. In this last exercise, we focus on how to use healthy doubt to assist you in your search for love, affirmation, and growth.

EXERCISE: Health of Relationship Questions

Ask yourself the following questions about a current relationship. If you're single, consider how these questions might guide your evaluation of a future dating relationship. Some of these questions are based on an exercise developed by Rajaee (2022, 44-45).

- Is the relationship caring? Do you treat each other with kindness and respect?

- Do you try to understand each other? Are you both willing to admit to mistakes and work on your shortcomings?

- Do you feel an emotional, physical, and (possibly) spiritual connection with your partner most of the time? Does your partner also show signs of having a deep connection with you?

- Do you have shared interests and a compatible, even similar, vision for the future?

- Are you and your partner able to communicate honestly about your true thoughts and feelings? Is each of you able to express yourself comfortably without fear or hesitation?

- Is there passion in the relationship, with your and your partner's intimacy and sexual wants and needs respected and often met?

- Do you have fun, laugh together, and enjoy each other's company?

- Are you able to disagree amicably and respectfully?

These questions are not easy to answer. You'll need to reflect deeply on your intimate relationship, using some level of doubt or questioning to arrive at an answer. But if most of your answers are affirmative, then your intimate relationship may be healthier than you think. And if this is the case, excessive doubt could easily lead you to make the wrong relationship decision.

Wrap-Up

Excessive doubt can undermine your efforts to establish and maintain a healthy intimate-partner relationship. In this chapter you were introduced to assessment tools that can help you determine if you have a healthy or unhealthy dose of relationship doubt. Your doubt may center on your own feelings and whether you truly love your partner, or you may be insecure about your partner's love. You may be still searching for that one and only special person, frightened that you are settling for less in any relationship. As you've seen, doubt can help you make important relationship decisions, or it can destroy your best efforts to find happiness in intimacy. If doubt is wreaking havoc with your love life, take heart. Change is possible when you stop striving for absolute certainty in your relationship. But for now, let's consider how excessive doubt can wreck another type of relationship: your spiritual connection with God or a universal spirit.

CHAPTER 8

Religious Doubt

Doubt is a common theme in religious teachings. If you are a religious or spiritual person, you've probably experienced doubt about the core teachings of your faith at one time or another. For some, however, doubt is a persistent questioning, an assault on the foundations of their faith that has left them feeling confused, anxious, and lost. If doubt is an unwelcome intrusion in your spiritual journey that is causing significant personal distress, this chapter is for you. Doubt can be a constructive state that leads to growth and renewal in your spiritual life, or it can be destructive, in some cases causing significant mental anguish.

If religious doubt is threatening your mental health, you're not alone. For centuries, sacred texts and wisdom literature have recognized the struggle with doubt and its potential to undermine belief and devotion. Here are a few selected quotes related to doubt from the Jewish, Christian, and Muslim traditions, respectively:

The term commonly applied to Jewish people is "B'nai Israel," the children of Israel. In the Torah we read "God said to him, your name is Jacob, but you will no longer be called Jacob; your name will be Israel. So he named him Israel" (New International Version 1995, 59). As Rabbi Cheryl Peretz (2005) noted in an online article, *Israel* literally means "one who struggles with God." We see here the recognition that doubt, uncertainty, and questioning are central features of the spiritual journey in Judaism.

But when he asks, he must believe and not doubt, because he who doubts is like a wave of the sea, blown and tossed by the wind. (James 1:6, New International Version 1995, 1,880)

The true believers are only those who believe in Allah and His Messenger, and afterward doubt not, but strive with their wealth and their lives for the cause of Allah. Such are the sincere. (Qur'an Al-Hujurat 49:15)

Throughout the ages theologians, philosophers, and religious leaders have wrestled with the problem of doubt. Moses, for example, questioned God's command that he lead his people out of Egypt (Exodus 3:11). Thomas, one of Jesus's original disciples, doubted initial reports of the resurrection (John 20:24–29). It is well-documented that Martin Luther, father of Protestantism, had moments of doubt about his call and salvation. More recently Mother Theresa wrote about her serious struggles with doubt and unbelief, and Pope Francis stated that everyone doubts, even he, but that doubt is not to be feared but embraced as part of one's spiritual journey (Wooden 2016).

> Doubt and uncertainty are integral to faith and belief. Without doubt there would be no need for faith.

If doubt is an inherent element of faith, why are so many people of faith troubled by their doubts? To answer this question, we'll delve into the complexities of religious doubt from a psychological perspective. We'll start with a deep dive into unhealthy doubt and exercises that will be useful for determining your own level of unhealthy religious or spiritual doubt. We'll then consider loss of conviction, the quintessential element in religious doubt, and conclude with a characterization of healthy, faith-enhancing doubt. But let's begin with the story of Celeste, whose unrelenting doubts about faith and religious practice caused significant mental health problems.

Celeste's Story: *Shattered by Doubt*

Celeste was raised in a strict, conservative Christian home. Throughout childhood, she accepted her church's dictates without question. She never challenged her parents' teaching that the only true path to salvation was through a life committed to Christ and his teachings. At the age of eight, Celeste made a personal decision to give her heart to Christ, was baptized, and later became a member of the church. After leaving home to attend college, however, Celeste began to experience doubt about God and the reality of her spiritual experiences. As a child, Celeste had developed a deep fear of Satan, hell, and God's punishment. For some unknown reason these fears started to resurface. One doubt came to the fore in her mind: *What if she was not in a right relationship with God? What if God was displeased with her?*

These doubts were especially distressing because Celeste didn't understand their origin. If she was doubting, maybe Satan—if Satan even existed—was trying to capture her soul. In response she read the Bible fervently, hoping to find the reassurance of salvation, and she prayed continually, pleading for God to take away the doubts, all to no avail. In fact, the opposite happened; the doubts became more extreme. She then wondered if she was so bad that she was beyond God's forgiveness. *Have I committed the unforgivable sin?* she asked herself, which is a common fear for some Christians that is derived from Jesus's words in Luke 12:10. Celeste wondered, Am I now doomed to eternal punishment?

Celeste's uncertainty about her inherent sinfulness and ruptured relationship with God drove her into deep personal despair. She could think of little else and so was forced to drop out of college because of failing grades. She rarely got a good night's sleep, and recurring nightmares were common. She withdrew from others, isolating herself in her bedroom and spending long hours surfing the Internet for answers. Nothing she read, and no pastoral counseling she received, could dispel her fear of God's abandonment. She could achieve no assurance of salvation. She stopped going to church, reading the Bible, and even praying because these triggered her obsessive doubts. But the avoidance intensified her guilt and the belief that she might be a child of the devil. Celeste started battling suicidal thoughts and eventually fell into a severe depression that required hospitalization.

For many people religious doubt is not merely a philosophical inquiry, a quest for truth. As is evident in Celeste's story, religious doubt can rock the very foundations of personal identity and security, causing the mental health of people of faith to deteriorate. In its most extreme form, they might go so far as to question whether they're inherently evil and so doomed to eternal damnation. To the unbeliever, these doubts seem nonsensical, but to people of faith they can be all too real and earth shattering.

Are religious or spiritual doubts causing you significant personal pain? You may already know the answer. Or perhaps your religious or spiritual doubts are distressing but you're not sure if they're contributing to feelings of anxiety, depression, or chronic guilt. The assessment tools in the next section will help you determine the seriousness of your religious or spiritual doubts.

More Than Simply Doubt

For the faithful, doubt cannot be avoided. Down through the centuries great spiritual minds have recognized that doubt is a double-edged sword. It can strengthen your belief and devotion, or it can cause a turning away from your faith tradition. Understanding your experiences of doubt is important to determining their effect on your spiritual journey. In the first exercise below, you'll delve into the central tenets of your faith, and in the second you'll assess the impact that doubt has on your psychological and spiritual well-being.

EXERCISE: Effort to Believe Scale

For each of the following core religious beliefs that are common to most faith traditions, circle the number that corresponds to how much you believe the statement.

Belief Statement	No Effort to Believe	Some Effort to Believe	Considerable Effort to Believe
I struggle to believe in God or a universal spirit.	0	1	2
I struggle to believe that the sacred text I read (Bible, Torah, Qur'an, etc.) is the inspired word of God.	0	1	2
I struggle to believe there is life after death.	0	1	2
I struggle to believe that I can live in peace and harmony with God or a universal spirit.	0	1	2
I struggle to believe that miracles occur or in the existence of supernatural phenomena (e.g., angels, demons).	0	1	2
I struggle to believe that I am inherently sinful and in need of God's mercy and forgiveness.	0	1	2
I struggle to believe there is only one truth or way to salvation.	0	1	2
I struggle to believe that my life is directed by God or a universal spirit.	0	1	2
I struggle to believe there is eternal punishment (hell) for those with insufficient belief and commitment.	0	1	2
I struggle to believe in an all-loving and compassionate God or universal spirit.	0	1	2
I struggle to believe there is an evil force or devil intent on separating me from God or the universal spirit.	0	1	2
I struggle to believe I can have a personal relationship with God or a universal spirit.	0	1	2

You'll notice the scale focuses on your *effort to believe*. It is not a measure of your strength of belief. A highly religious person could score 0 if they had no trouble believing each statement. Likewise, an irreligious person could score 0 because they don't believe any of the statements, and so there's no effort to believe. However, a person of faith might score much higher if they're struggling to believe many of the statements.

If you scored a 1 or 2 on four or more statements, then you may be experiencing moderate to high levels of religious or spiritual doubt. But this doesn't mean it's a problem for you. You also need to consider how religious or spiritual doubt affects your quality of life, which the next exercise will help you assess.

> Serious religious doubt often occurs as a struggle to believe many of the tenets central to your faith tradition.

EXERCISE: Impact of Doubt Worksheet

Indicate whether the following negative effects associated with excessive religious or spiritual doubt apply to you by placing a checkmark in the appropriate column.

Statement	True	False
I pray for my sins and wrongdoings to be forgiven many times a day.		
I often feel that I'm displeasing or disappointing God.		
I struggle with intense feelings of guilt.		
I often have immoral thoughts and images in my head that I don't want.		
As hard as I try, I don't feel at peace with God.		
I feel defeated by temptations that I can't resist.		
I experience evil or blasphemous thoughts that I can't suppress despite my best efforts.		
I am fearful of hell and God's punishment.		
I avoid all religious practices (e.g., going to church, reading the Bible, praying) because I find them distressing.		
I struggle to control unwanted, immoral, even disgusting sexual thoughts and fantasies.		

Statement	True	False
I know God loves me, but I can't feel this love and acceptance.		
As hard as I try, I do not feel a sense of conviction that I'm right with God.		

Did you check many of the statements as true? If six or more apply to you, then religious or spiritual doubt may be having a significant negative effect on your faith and personal life. Celeste would mark many of these statements as true. She was convinced she was displeasing God, was fearful of hell and punishment, felt intense guilt, avoided all religious practice, and had no conviction that her relationship with God was right. So oppressive and disrupting were these doubts that Celeste considered ending her life to deal with her inner turmoil.

> Religious doubt is most serious when it causes significant personal distress and becomes a barrier to spiritual growth and development.

Has your work in these exercises indicated that religious or spiritual doubt is a more serious problem than you realized? It may be clear to you that doubt is having a negative impact on your mental health and quality of life. Fortunately, it doesn't have to be this way. Many people of great spiritual depth have harnessed their doubt to enrich and deepen their faith tradition. But before doubt can have a positive influence, you need to learn what drove it in the opposite direction.

Loss of Conviction

Debilitating religious doubt most often reflects a loss of conviction. Recall in chapter 3 that I defined *conviction* as "a deep, internal sense of certainty." Conviction is a characteristic of moral, ethical, and religious beliefs. If you lose a sense of conviction in your religious or spiritual beliefs, your doubts can feel overwhelming. Celeste lost her conviction that God had forgiven her sins, and that she was in a right relationship with the Divine. She no longer had a "feeling of knowing" that she was accepted by God. She couldn't sense God's presence in her life. And so her doubt intensified. It didn't help that Celeste was trying to find conviction in the wrong places, such as by finding a convincing argument or by having a defining spiritual experience.

Information Seeking

When we doubt, it's only natural to seek information, an argument, or other evidence that settles the doubt. If you are uncertain whether you offended a friend, you'd probably ask them directly as a way of disconfirming your doubt. But doubts about moral or spiritual beliefs are much different because they involve values and beliefs that transcend our worldly existence. Because of this transcendent nature, disconfirming evidence is hard to come by. You can strengthen your religious belief, but you can't use information, reason, or a particular argument to eradicate *all doubt*.

Let's consider the difference between a *feeling of knowing* and a *knowing of knowing*. For example, you know with absolute certainty that gravity, consciousness, and death are real. You continuously experience the effects of gravity (If you doubt it, try jumping up and down!), you know you're alive in this moment, and you know you'll eventually succumb to death. All these examples fall within the realm of knowing of knowing.

Now consider belief in God or a universal spirit, life after death, and forgiveness of sins. They are much different than gravity, consciousness, and death because the religious realm is transcendent. We can achieve a feeling of knowing about these things, but that will not eradicate all doubts we might have. This is why we can talk of having conviction (a feeling of knowing) about our moral and religious beliefs, but we don't have conviction about gravity, consciousness, or death. One deals with the natural world, the other the supernatural.

> Loss of conviction in religious and moral beliefs can occur when you strive for the impossible—that is, when you try to eradicate all doubt through knowledge and reason.

People experience a loss of conviction when they strive for a knowing of knowing for things for which they can only have a feeling of knowing. Are you caught in the information-seeking game, erroneously thinking your doubts can be eliminated through evidence, reason, or argument? The next exercise gives you an opportunity to consider how information seeking might be feeding your loss of conviction.

EXERCISE: Looking for Answers

Start by writing down the religious or spiritual belief you doubt most. It should be your most troubling religious or spiritual doubt. Next, using your imagination, write out what evidence you'd need to become completely, absolutely certain about the truthfulness of the religious belief. This perfect, absolutely compelling information, reason, or argument would confirm the belief and erase all doubt. First, consider Celeste's responses.

My greatest religious/spiritual doubt: That God has forgiven my sinful thoughts, actions, and intentions, and I am now in a right relationship with the Divine.

Write a paragraph describing the information, reason, argument, or evidence you would need for your greatest religious/spiritual doubt to be eliminated.

I think I would need to hear an audible voice that I knew was God. I would know it was not my thoughts or Satan trying to deceive me. It would sound like God, and he would say, "I forgive you absolutely, completely, without reservation." I would then feel an overwhelming peace and comfort from hearing the voice. Or, I would have a vision; an angel would stand in my presence, put her arm around me, and say, "You are forgiven." I would feel such calm flood through my body that there would be no doubt that I was not hallucinating but having a real visitation from the supernatural world. Or, I'd have a miracle happen in my life that could not be explained by the world's greatest minds except that it was an act of God.

My greatest religious/spiritual doubt: _____

_____

_____

_____

Write a paragraph describing the information, reason, argument, or evidence you would need for your greatest religious/spiritual doubt to be eliminated.

_____

_____

_____

_____

_____

_____

_____

_____

_____

_____

Take a moment to review what you've written. Is it possible to obtain the information you've written out? Do you think even if you found this information that you'd never doubt again? Celeste quickly recognized the impossibility of her criteria. Is God really going to speak to her in an audible voice, or will she be visited by an angel? It is easy to see from her narrative that Celeste will never receive the ultimate disconfirming evidence that would quench her doubt.

Emotion Seeking

Emotion is an important part of any religious or spiritual experience. When people of like-minded faith gather together, they sing, dance, listen to music, and engage in various emotion-laden activities and rituals. Religious and spiritual life are full of emotion. And since we are emotional beings, a truly authentic spiritual experience will elicit a variety of emotions, such as joy, excitement, surprise, awe, elation, calm, peace, and love to name but a few. Not only should we expect to have strong feelings during our spiritual experiences, but emotional expression is an important part of worship in most faith traditions.

Problems arise when people seek a certain emotional experience to regain conviction and diminish religious/spiritual doubt. Since conviction is an inner or subjective sense of certainty, you might think that having a particular emotional experience would be the ultimate proof of your connection with the Divine. *If I could feel a deep sense of peace and calm, then I would be certain that I am right with God. If I prayed and joy burst forth, causing tears of gratitude and praise, then I would be convinced there is a God who cares for me.* In your spiritual journey, have you had an emotional experience that made you feel close to God or a universal spirit? If you are now experiencing distressing levels of religious or spiritual doubt, do you think that re-creating a previous emotional experience could strengthen your conviction in your beliefs?

> Emotions are ephemeral, so they are not the answer to lost conviction.

In Celeste's faith tradition, the evidence of a deep connection with God was an emotion-laden experience called "baptism of the Holy Spirit." This often occurred in highly energetic worship services involving enthusiastic singing, clapping, and dancing. Sometimes people were so overcome with intense joy, excitement, and awe that they spontaneously spoke in tongues. It was during these moments of spiritual ecstasy that Celeste had felt truly connected to God in her early teens. In college, when she started doubting her relationship with God and worrying that Satan was drawing her away from her faith, personal experiences of the baptism of the Holy Spirit dwindled in frequency and intensity until there were none. It was at this point that she stopped going to church. Celeste was convinced that if she could get back to these ecstatic experiences, her distressing religious doubts would melt away. If, like Celeste, you think that a particular emotional experience might eradicate your doubts and strengthen your conviction, complete the following exercise.

EXERCISE: Reaching for Nirvana

In the space below describe the "ideal" emotional or spiritual experience that would reestablish conviction in your religious or spiritual beliefs and practices, then answer the following questions.

_____

_____

_____

_____

_____

_____

_____

_____

To solve all your religious doubts, would this emotional experience have to be continuous, or could it fluctuate? If not continuous, how many times would you need to have the experience for it to have a positive effect on doubt?

_____

_____

_____

Does this experience always have to be the same, or can it vary?

_____

Have you considered how life circumstances (for example, the death of a loved one, family conflict, life-threatening illness) might affect this experience?

_____

_____

Having finished this exercise, can you see that an emotional or a spiritual experience may not be the answer to your loss of conviction? The doubts will return, sometimes with greater intensity. If seeking answers through knowledge and reason or reassurance through a particular emotion is not the answer for religious doubt, then what can you do? There is an alternative: faith-based doubt.

Faith-Based Doubt

Doubt is an inescapable part of faith. Without doubt, faith cannot exist. But as we have seen, doubt can become a destroyer of faith, leaving the most devout person in a state of personal crisis. If faith and doubt are symbiotic states of mind, then surely there must be a healthy form of religious or spiritual doubt.

To consider this possibility, let's reflect on the meaning of "faith." We start by recognizing that religious or spiritual faith is a strongly held belief or trust in that which cannot be verified by empirical evidence. Perhaps the most famous verse on faith for Christian believers is "Now faith is being sure of what we hope for and certain of what we do not see" (Hebrews 11:1, New International Version 1995, 1,870). The last part of this verse, "of what we do not see," reflects that the unknown is an integral part of faith. Uncertainty is how we relate to the unknown. How we deal with this uncertainty (doubt) determines whether our faith (hope) is strengthened or shattered. The following exercise lists characteristics of a healthy form of doubt that can increase your trust and confidence in the tenets of your faith tradition.

> Because faith focuses on what is unknowable, doubt is inescapable to the believer.

EXERCISE: Healthy Doubt Checklist

The following statements reflect a positive, healthy doubt that can enhance your belief in your faith tradition. Place a checkmark next to the statements you agree with. If you don't agree or are unsure, don't place a checkmark next to the statement.

- ☐ Through doubt I acknowledge the unknown and the mystery of life.

- ☐ I'm reminded of my limited capacity to understand everything when I doubt.

- ☐ When I doubt, I focus on raising my tolerance of uncertainty for that which I cannot know or control.

- ☐ Doubt helps me focus on faith (a hope for what I cannot see).

- ☐ Doubt is a natural aspect of the human brain as it tries to grasp the unknown.

- ☐ I use doubt as a cue to restate trust in my religious or spiritual beliefs.

- ☐ I continue to practice the activities and rituals of my faith tradition even during times of doubt.

- ☐ I exercise kindness and compassion toward myself when I doubt.

- ☐ I do not fear or deny doubt, rather I embrace it.

- ☐ The questions associated with doubt have brought me insights and a new understanding of my faith.

Were you unable to check off many of the statements? If so, consider how you might make these statements part of your faith journey. Ask questions and seek advice from your religious leaders and authoritative writings to determine how you can use doubt to enrich your spiritual life.

Wrap-Up

Doubt can feel like the destroyer of faith. If you are a person of faith, a loss of conviction in your spiritual beliefs and values can be upsetting enough to threaten your mental health. It can feel like you've lost a sense of who you are, and perhaps doubt has thrown you into a state of depression and intolerable guilt, as it did Celeste. But doubt is an inescapable part of faith.

Did you conclude from this chapter that you suffer from a toxic form of religious doubt? Have you lost conviction in your spiritual beliefs and practices because you seek an unattainable level of knowing or an experience that is all too transitory? As you've seen, there is a form of doubt that can strengthen your beliefs and enrich your spiritual journey. It requires that you turn doubt on its head and see it as a reminder that you can embrace the unknowable and celebrate it as integral to life itself. We'll turn now to therapeutic strategies you can use to overcome your struggle with excessive doubt and uncertainty.

PART 3

The Other Side of Doubt

CHAPTER 9

Doubt the Doubt

Candice and Michael, both in their late thirties, were facing a crisis in their relationship. Michael wanted to start a family, but Candice wasn't sure she wanted children. Each of them had good reasons for their position, but every time they tried to talk about the issue, they ended in a heated argument. They weren't able to listen to each other because each stood firmly in their viewpoint. The issue had been festering for years, and the sense of urgency caused by the passage of time was making matters worse.

Candice had doubts about pregnancy and a baby because she was highly invested in a rewarding, successful career as a corporate lawyer. Although many of her friends juggled career and motherhood, they always seemed so stressed, and there was no question that their careers took a hit. Candice was raised in a single-parent household, and although her mother had done the best she could, Candice's childhood had been difficult. As a teenager she vowed never to have children. Candice doubted whether she had the compassion and empathy necessary to be a good mother. *What if we have a difficult baby who never stops fussing or crying?* Candice didn't think she could take the additional stress.

But Candice could also see Michael's point of view. Would they regret not having children as they got older? Who would look out for them in their senior years when they were in declining health? And children did seem to give great joy, meaning, and purpose to her friends. She would miss out on all this if she followed her doubt, which seemed to be telling her, *Don't do it. Better to maintain the status quo than risk having a baby.*

Can you empathize with Candice? Are you facing a similar dilemma? Perhaps it's not about having children: *Should I quit my job and go back to school? Should we get married? Should we buy a bigger house? Should I retire or keep working?* And the list goes on. For each of these examples, and others, doubt can reign supreme. You may feel like doubt is leading you in a particular direction, as Candice did. But putting too much stock in your doubts can result in a dangerous misinterpretation that can lead you astray.

> Overinterpreting the meaning and significance of doubt can lead to poor decision making.

This chapter presents a series of intervention strategies I call "doubt the doubt." Their purpose is to help us correct our faulty interpretation of significance for our excessive doubt. First we'll need to catch the automatic misinterpretation and replace it with a balanced, more accurate understanding of the situation. You can also directly question the doubt. The ultimate goal is to acknowledge that doubt only delays decision making. Some work on the problem of inferential confusion, as discussed in chapter 6, is needed to bolster efforts to doubt the doubt; several intervention strategies address this error. Another way to *doubt the doubt* is to identify any reasoning errors associated with your tendency to overinterpret the significance of doubt. Being aware of these errors will help you correct the misinterpretation bias. And finally, we'll consider how you can take action despite having doubt.

Catch and Release

You may be familiar with the term "catch and release" from recreational fishing. It's the practice of catching a fish and then immediately releasing it back into the water as a conservation measure. We can borrow this term and apply it to your doubt. It describes a two-stage process in which you first acknowledge you're having doubt—that is, catch your initial automatic interpretation of the doubt—and then release the doubt by offering an alternative interpretation of its significance.

To use this intervention effectively, it helps to recall our definition of doubt from the book's introduction and how doubt is not inherently significant. *Doubt* is the state of being aware of various possibilities because of heightened uncertainty about the best decision or action. Doubt often results in a delay in making a decision. So, doubt cannot tell you what to do, it can only suggest that you delay a decision or an action.

> It is an error to assume that doubt is providing some answer when in reality it is only telling you to wait, to gather more information before making a decision.

The next exercise presents the catch and release intervention. It's the place to begin when you need to correct the error of overinterpreting the significance of doubt.

EXERCISE: Reinterpreting Your Doubt

This exercise has two parts. First, write down your initial, automatic thoughts about the meaning or significance of a doubt that you wrote about in the book's introduction. Write about what the doubt *feels like* to you. These first thoughts about the doubt may seem quite irrational when you reconsider them more seriously. Take a look at Candice's example for ideas on how to identify your first interpretation.

My first reaction to the doubt is to assume it means I'm not ready to have a baby. If I have all these doubts, maybe I'm not cut out to be a mother. I might be one of those career-minded women who can't divide her time between work and home. I'd find the whole thing way too stressful and then regret ever having a baby. Michael says he'll take equal responsibility, but I'm not so sure. If I was full of resentment, then I would end up ruining the child's life. In all, the doubt makes me feel like I'm unsuited for parenthood.

My initial interpretation of doubt:

_____

_____

_____

_____

_____

Now, take time to analyze the doubt thoughtfully. This process should capture a more realistic interpretation of the doubt, what *you think* the doubt can tell you about a decision or past action. This interpretation should be based on what your senses tell you, what is common sense. Again, take a look at Candice's example before completing your alternative interpretation.

Of course, I'm having these doubts because I've never been pregnant. Doubt is a reaction to uncertainty, and I'm feeling very uncertain about the future. I can't even imagine being a working mother with a supportive spouse. So, my doubts feel stronger because the future seems more unpredictable, more uncertain as a first-time mother. The doubt isn't an indication of my ability to mother. It's only telling me to think it through carefully, to be aware of my reasons for and against getting pregnant. These reasons can't make me more certain because I can't know the future. But fairly soon I'll need to make a decision whether or not to accept the same risk that millions upon millions of women take when they get pregnant.

My alternative interpretation of doubt:

_____

_____

_____

_____

_____

The preceding intervention is the first step in learning to doubt the doubt. It is not an easy strategy to master. At first it will feel forced and quite academic, but the more you practice with a variety of doubts, the easier it will get. Eventually, you'll develop your catch and release skills. Instead of buying into your initial interpretation of the doubt (how it feels), you'll quickly replace it with a more realistic, alternative interpretation. The doubt will begin to feel less significant because you'll be reminding yourself that doubt does not necessarily lead you to the truth or what will happen.

Catch and release is not the only way to doubt the doubt. The next intervention focuses on using doubt to make a more accurate prediction of what could happen.

Correct the Possibility Error

In chapter 6 you were introduced to the concept of inferential confusion as a contributor to obsessive doubt. You may recall that it involves treating what is possible as highly probable. One example I used is cooking dinner for guests. You may recall that Kali was worried she had contaminated vegetables with raw chicken and that her cooking would sicken her guests. The doubt played in her mind, and her anxiety grew. In this example, Kali was treating a possibility (*My cooking could poison my dinner guests*) as a probability (*My guests are likely to get sick from my cooking*). This confusing what is possible with what is most likely is another way to misinterpret the significance of your doubt. Correcting this error, then, is another way to doubt the doubt.

> You're more likely to misinterpret the significance of your doubt if you treat every imaginable possibility as if it will happen.

One way to work on correcting the possibility error is with an exercise introduced by O'Connor and Aardema (2012), which I call the Imagination vs. Reality Worksheet. It involves identifying all the possible outcomes that run through your mind when you have a doubt. Next, you consider all the reality-based information you have about whatever it is you're doubting. This is the real-world evidence—information coming from your senses, including common sense—that supports the doubt. (You completed a similar exercise, the Inferential Confusion Bias, with five hypothetical scenarios in chapter 6. In the following exercise, you'll apply the same approach to your current doubts.)

EXERCISE: Imagination vs. Reality Worksheet

In the first column, record the past actions, decisions, or beliefs that you doubt. Next, write down everything you imagine could happen in relation to the doubting concerns. These possibilities are what drive your doubts. In the third column, write down what you actually know about the past actions, decisions, or beliefs that you doubt. What are some commonsense views of the issues? What reliable sensory information do you have about the things that you doubt? The first row is an example. (This and other worksheets are available for download at this book's website, http://www.newharbinger.com/55756.)

Doubt	Possibilities (What I imagine could happen.)	Real-World Information (What my senses tell me.)
Should I sign on to this online dating platform for older adults?	• I might not get any swipes, and this would be devastating. • I reach out to people and no one replies; again, very devastating. • I start communicating and the person becomes rude and insulting. • I have a series of very awkward conversations online. • I'm filled with anxiety with the first face-to-face meeting. • I meet the love of my life.	• One of my friends had a good experience with online dating; she met a couple of interesting people but didn't pursue other contacts. • I have another friend who had a disappointing experience; she had very few matches, and they all were inappropriate. • I don't know anyone who's gotten into trouble with connections made online; it seems that most fizzle out because of different interests or incompatibility. • Overall, the most usual outcome for older adults is a series of poor matches or no response, but sometimes you get lucky.

Doubt	Possibilities (What I imagine could happen.)	Real-World Information (What my senses tell me.)

Doubt	Possibilities (What I imagine could happen.)	Real-World Information (What my senses tell me.)

Take a moment to review your answers. What do you notice? If your answers are anything like the example, most of the possibilities you imagine are much darker, more threatening, than the real-world information. If you pay more attention to your imagined possibilities, the doubts will feel more significant. But if you focus on the commonsense, real-world information you recorded in the third column, you'll be able to correct your misinterpretations of the significance of the doubts. You'll begin to doubt the doubt.

Like the previous exercise, this intervention will feel unnatural at first. You'll need to add new information to the real-world column as it comes to you. When you find yourself doubting, take out this worksheet and remind yourself of the real-world information you have at hand. Ask yourself if it's better to accept the real-world, commonsense information in the third column or to focus on your imagination in the second column. If you decide to accept reality, what your five senses are telling you, you'll be in a better position to doubt the doubt.

Getting snared by imaginative possibilities will cause you to exaggerate the significance of your doubt. The remedy is to focus on reality, what O'Connor and Aardema (2012) call "reality sensing." Doubt will become less intense, less significant, because you'll be using common sense, what's available to you in the here and now, to judge your doubts. They will become less important to making decisions and for dealing with past actions and beliefs. Using the Imagination vs. Reality Worksheet will help you correct the misinterpretation of doubt. There is another version of this exercise to supplement the work you've already completed. It focuses on instances of normal doubt, times when you didn't exaggerate the significance of the doubt.

> Doubt feels acceptable, like a normal experience, when you rely on what your senses are telling you about the real world.

EXERCISE: Normalized Doubt Worksheet

In the first column, write down times when you had doubt and the experience didn't feel intense or distressing. Next, imagine the possible outcomes you'd have to think about to misinterpret the significance of the doubt to make it distressing. In the final column, record the commonsense, real-world information that enabled you to realistically interpret the significance and thereby normalize the doubt. The first row provides an example from Candice.

Doubt	Possibilities (What I imagine could happen.)	Real-World Information (What my senses tell me.)
Is this quarterly report good enough, or should I spend more time on it?	· I leave out important information that invalidates the entire report. · I make mistakes and others judge me negatively. · I'm reprimanded for turning in a substandard report. · I lose my job.	· I really can't spend more time on the report; my other work will suffer and I'll miss deadlines. · I've written numerous quarterly reports before and they've never been substandard. · Changes are always needed, and we are given time to make them before the report is finalized.

Why do you think doubt felt quite normal in these circumstances but not in others? Is it because you paid more attention to what your senses told you than the imagined possibilities? Candice questioned whether she had spent enough time on the quarterly report. But this uncertainty, the doubt, didn't get out of hand because she focused on the real-world information in the third column. The doubt didn't become a significant experience, so she was able to turn her attention to more pressing work responsibilities. Were your normal experiences of doubt similar to hers? You can learn to doubt the doubt—that is, correct the misinterpretation of significance you see in excessive doubt—by understanding how you focus on reality when you experience normal doubt.

Thinking Errors

For decades, CBT therapists have known that we're more likely to commit errors in how we think about our self and the world we experience when we're depressed or anxious (Clark and Beck 2010). The same is probably true for excessive doubt. Although the necessary research has not been done, it makes sense that you're more likely to commit these same thinking errors when your doubt gets out of hand. If so, catching yourself making these errors and correcting them could be another way to dial back doubt. The next exercise provides a checklist of thinking errors that can be used when you're working on doubting the doubt.

EXERCISE: The Thinking Error Checklist

Think back to times when you experienced excessive doubt—doubts about past actions, decisions, or core beliefs. What types of thinking errors were present in your doubt? Place a checkmark beside the thinking errors that most commonly appear in your doubting experiences.

Catastrophizing	Thinking the worst is more likely to happen than is realistic.
All or nothing	Thinking in absolute terms; something is either completely present or absent.
Fortune telling	Assuming your predictions about the future are accurate and likely to come true.
Emotional reasoning	Assuming the doubt is more accurate because it feels so distressing.
Personalization	Thinking you have greater control over events than is realistic and so are to blame for unfortunate outcomes.
Tunnel vision	A narrow focus on certain aspects of a situation (usually the negative) while ignoring other aspects (usually the positive).

Were some errors more prominent in your doubt than others? If you had difficulty recalling past experiences of intense doubt, keep a diary of your doubts over the next two weeks. When recording a doubting episode, review this checklist and mark which errors are present in your doubt. Practice identifying the thinking errors when you doubt. Just naming the errors will cause you to automatically correct your thinking. It's like catching an error in your calculations. You'd hardly proceed with the calculation until you corrected the error. And when you identify and correct your thinking errors, you're also correcting your tendency to overthink doubt, which is another way to doubt the doubt.

> When you catch errors in your thinking, you're less likely to misinterpret the significance of your doubt.

Fortune telling, emotional reasoning, and tunnel vision were Candice's most common thinking errors. When having doubts about motherhood, she had a biased view of the future. She felt like she knew the future, and it would be overwhelming and suffocating. The distress she felt when having the doubts made them seem more real. Dwelling on the imagined possibilities made the negative aspects of parenting more real, whereas the positive elements were harder to grasp. Once Candice became aware of her thinking errors, she was able to realign her doubts so she could stop misinterpreting their significance. Instead, she worked on adopting a more realistic, balanced perspective that considered both the positive and negative aspects of parenting.

Acting Against Doubt

Actions speak louder than words! How often do you recite this phrase to yourself? It's a truism we use when judging the character and intentions of others. But it also has great relevance for addressing doubt. If you really want to get a handle on your doubt, you have to take action. Doubting the doubt requires you to respond differently when you're caught in the throes of excessive doubt. Overinterpreting the significance of doubt will be your natural response when doubt has become a problem. You need to develop an action plan that allows you to do the opposite—to downplay in your mind the meaning and significance of excessive doubt.

> You need a plan that requires you to take action in spite of lingering feelings of doubt.

EXERCISE: A Plan of Action Against Doubt

Use the space below to write out a step-by-step plan that you'll follow when making a decision, recalling a past action, or questioning a core belief that involves a heightened level of doubt. Be specific about what you'll do even though you have doubts. Your action plan should lead you to do the opposite of what you'd do if you listened to your doubts. Be intentional about following this plan regardless of your doubts. First, consider Candice's action plan concerning her doubts about having a baby.

I've come to realize my doubts about having a baby will never completely evaporate. I've been indecisive about this issue for too long. I'm approaching my mid-thirties, and time is not on my side. So, I'll give myself another six months. During that time, I'll talk to three to five friends and work colleagues about their experience of deciding whether or not to have children. I'll specifically ask about their doubts and how they dealt with indecision. I'll also do some more online searches for articles about handling the stress and challenges of work and having a baby. I will also inquire about daycare, maternity benefits at work, and any accommodations available to working mothers. I'll have several heart-to-heart conversations with Michael about his ability to live with my decision whether or not to get pregnant. After six months, I will make my decision and stick to it. I know I'll still have doubts whatever I decide, but I'll let the doubt sit there—be present—when making the decision.

Make sure you create a plan that is realistic. Can you actually see yourself following your action plan? Notice that every step in Candice's plan involves actions she can take even if she feels doubtful. The main point is to engage in acts that result in some resolution despite your continuing doubts. Acting in a constructive way while still having doubts weakens the misinterpretation of significance. Acting against the doubt is a powerful intervention for doubting the doubt.

Wrap-Up

Doubt can be a powerful experience that's hard to ignore. Doubt is often helpful, stopping us from making a rash decision or informing us of past mistakes or indiscretions. But it can also be excessive and counterproductive, causing unnecessary personal distress and a reduced ability to function. It is during these times that we must rise above the doubt, to act despite its presence, acknowledging that we have a tendency to misinterpret the significance of doubt.

Practicing doubt the doubt interventions is one way to curtail the negative impact doubt has on your life. It begins with recognizing when you're overinterpreting the significance of doubt and replacing this interpretation with a more realistic meaning for the doubt. The most effective strategy for correcting the misinterpretation of doubt is shifting your attention from imagined possibilities to the real-world information derived from your senses. This process also addresses the problem of inferential confusion that people often experience with excessive doubt. Developing a greater sensitivity to the thinking errors that are present when you're doubting, and implementing an action plan for dealing with the issues driving your doubt, will strengthen the skills you need to doubt the doubt. In the following chapter we'll explore another intervention for overcoming excessive doubt: improving your tolerance of uncertainty, which is a core feature of doubt.

CHAPTER 10

Living with Uncertainty

Uncertainty is the one certainty in this life. There is no escaping it. And as you learned from chapter 1, uncertainty is the core feature of doubt. But people differ greatly in their ability to tolerate uncertainty. Those who are less tolerant of uncertainty will have a greater problem with doubt than people with a higher tolerance. So, raising your uncertainty tolerance is an important intervention for overcoming debilitating doubt.

Shauna had a low tolerance for uncertainty. She tried to keep her life as routine, predictable, and controllable as possible. Any novel experience or ambiguous situation was anxiety provoking for her because it triggered the fear of the unknown. Shauna's low uncertainty tolerance caused her to miss out on the excitement, pleasures, and sense of accomplishment that give us meaning and life satisfaction. For example, Shauna rarely traveled because she associated it with so many uncertainties. She found it difficult to socialize or make new friends because she felt uncertain about whether she'd be accepted. She never joined social activities such as dancing, Pilates, hiking, or book clubs because the unfamiliar filled her with a sense of uncertainty. She avoided social media because posting a response might elicit a negative reaction. Uncertainty led to her avoidance. She was saving for a downpayment on a condominium but avoided investments that would give her a better return for fear of stock market volatility. It is easy to see how Shauna's low uncertainty tolerance caused many doubts that greatly reduced her quality of life.

> Learning to tolerate a reasonable level of uncertainty is key to overcoming your problems with doubt.

This chapter offers a series of cognitive behavioral interventions that can strengthen your tolerance of uncertainty. If you scored high on the Measure of Uncertainty Tolerance in chapter 1, you'll want to spend extra time working with this chapter's interventions. As a person with low tolerance for uncertainty, these interventions will be crucial to overcoming paralyzing, excessive doubt.

I discussed some of these interventions in my book *This Is What Anxiety Looks Like* (Clark 2024). The Uncertainty Tolerance Log will have you explore whether your level of uncertainty tolerance is greater than you think. The Certainty Gradient will ask you to think of certainty in terms of degrees rather than as present or absent. With The Novelty Experiences Worksheet, you'll learn how to introduce increasing levels of novelty and change into your daily living. And finally, I'll introduce a couple of intervention strategies that can help you tolerate the distress of uncertainty.

Tolerance of Uncertainty in Everyday Living

Certainty is the opposite of uncertainty. Excessive and distressing doubt is driven by efforts to reduce an intolerable feeling of uncertainty about past actions or decisions (see chapter 1). In your efforts to reduce uncertainty, you are also trying to gain a greater level of certainty in your activities and decision making. But what if you're trying to gain an unrealistic level of certainty? This is another way of saying that your relationship with certainty and uncertainty is driving your persistent and distressing doubt. Shauna's low tolerance for feeling uncertain meant that she strove for an unattainable level of certainty (or reassurance) that everything would turn out fine if she tried something new. But what Shauna was forgetting was that she did many things throughout the day without absolute certainty. She tolerated uncertainty and didn't expect an absolute level of certainty and didn't realize it.

> We are able to function in our daily living because we tolerate uncertainty. We achieve a feeling of knowing an outcome even though objectively, the outcome can't be known with absolute certainty.

Is it possible you have more tolerance for uncertainty than you realize, even though you can't be absolutely certain of outcomes? Take a moment to consider your daily activities. You get up in the morning and assume you're well enough to go to work. You take the same route to work and assume you'll get there on time. You send emails, text, set up meetings, post material online, and perform a host of other tasks, trusting you're doing them correctly. You see your doctor and assume the test results are accurate and were not mixed up with another person's. You do online banking, trusting that your transactions are secure. But nothing is 100 percent certain. You make assumptions, you trust it'll all work out, and it generally does. You are *exercising* a tolerance for uncertainty even if you're not aware of it. In order to live in this high-tech, integrated society, we are forced to trust systems and other people.

Is it possible you have more tolerance for uncertainty than you realize? The next exercise gives you an opportunity to explore the boundaries of your uncertainty tolerance in daily living.

EXERCISE: Uncertainty Tolerance Log

Think about all the tasks you manage each day and write down five to six of them in the first column. (See the previous paragraph for examples.) For each task think about what could go wrong and write it in the second column. Then write down the reasons why you're able to tolerate the possibility that something could go wrong. An example from Shauna is in the first row.

Daily Tasks	What Could Go Wrong and How I Tolerated the Uncertainty
I use autodeposits and automatic e-payments for most of my monthly bills.	I suppose my biweekly salary might not get deposited or my bills won't get paid on time because of a technical software problem with the bank. I cope with this uncertainty by telling myself that (a) it's very unlikely to happen; (b) if it did happen, it's a mistake that I can get corrected, although it would be a big hassle; and (c) what choice do I have? I need the convenience of online banking.

Daily Tasks	What Could Go Wrong and How I Tolerated the Uncertainty

Are you surprised that you're able to tolerate uncertainty with many of the tasks of daily living? What you tell yourself about something going wrong, about the uncertainty that something bad could happen, determines whether you're okay with tolerating some uncertainty and not requiring an unattainable level of knowing the outcome. And if you can tolerate the uncertainty, you're not likely to experience excessive doubt. Shauna didn't waste a lot of time doubting her banking transactions because she learned to trust the banking system and her ability to execute transactions correctly. Could mistakes happen? Could she get hacked? Absolutely! But she learned to tolerate this uncertainty and so did not doubt herself.

Based on what you discovered with the Uncertainty Tolerance Log, use the next worksheet to apply the same reasoning to your intolerance of uncertainty and doubt.

EXERCISE: Uncertainty Worksheet

List some of your most recent doubts in the first column. (You can use the doubts you listed in the Doubts About Past Actions and Decisions, Experiences of Indecision, and Doubts About Core Beliefs exercises in the introduction.) In the second column state what you fear could go wrong. This is the outcome that drives your doubt and uncertainty. In the third column list several ways you can think about the situation that will help you tolerate the uncertainty related to the undesirable outcome. You may want to review the strategies you listed in the Uncertainty Tolerance Log. An example from Shauna is provided in the first row.

Doubt	What I Fear Could Go Wrong	How I Can Tolerate the Uncertainty
Should I sign up for Pilates?	I could embarrass myself. I'd feel such shame and never return. It would be another defeat.	1. I don't know what will happen. It could be better than I expect, or it could be worse. 2. What's the most embarrassing thing I could do? Maybe not keep up with the class. 3. I don't know these people; they have no role in my life; they'll have no interest in me. 4. I can go once and never return. It's entirely optional.

Doubt	What I Fear Could Go Wrong	How I Can Tolerate the Uncertainty

Did you discover new reasons to tolerate the uncertainty associated with your excessive doubt? How you think about the possibility of undesirable outcomes determines your ability to tolerate uncertainty and relinquish efforts to attain unrealistic levels of certainty about the outcome. Shauna had real doubts about joining Pilates. It was impossible to know how it would go. She feared the uncertainty of attending that first class and the possibility of suffering acute embarrassment. But then she thought further about the uncertainty and realized she was exaggerating a potentially undesired outcome. Did you find the same held true with your doubts when you evaluated them?

> Uncertainty tolerance can be improved by seeing the feared outcome associated with your doubt in more realistic terms.

Keeping an Uncertainty Tolerance Log and then using what you learn to change your thinking with the Uncertainty Worksheet is one way to strengthen your tolerance for uncertainty.

Degrees of Certainty

Does certainty feel like it's all or nothing? Either you have a sense of certainty and life goes on with little doubt, or you feel distressed by unrelenting doubt because you're racked with uncertainty about undesirable possibilities. The truth is that uncertainty is neither all present nor all absent. Instead, our sense of certainty occurs on a gradient.

Lots of phenomena occur on a gradient, such as temperature (Fahrenheit or Celsius), measurements (inches, feet, weight), and the like. The experience of pain is often expressed as a gradient, such as when your doctor asks you to rate your pain from 0 to 10. So, too, does our sense of certainty occur as a gradient, fluctuating between the extremes of 0% and 100%. In any situation we can say, "I have XX% certainty that such and such is going to happen."

To illustrate this gradient, imagine you've had your car for many years and it's likely you will have costly repairs to contend with soon. Do you keep your old car and absorb the costly repairs, or do you trade it in with the possibility that the car payments will stretch your monthly budget? You have lots of doubt about what the right decision is. If you have high tolerance for uncertainty, you accept that you can't know the future. So, you make do with the information you have and make a decision. If you have low tolerance for uncertainty, you continue to seek more and more information, hoping to reduce your feeling of uncertainty. And so you dither, feeling more stressed from not being able to make a decision. To use our gradient analogy, the high-tolerance person needs to feel only 40% certain to make a decision; the low-tolerance person needs to feel 80% certain, which

> We experience varying levels of certainty depending on the situation. If you have low tolerance for uncertainty, you will need a higher percentage of certainty to avoid doubt.

means they'll continue to search for additional information that pushes their feeling of certainty to 80%.

The Certainty Gradient below is a powerful yet complicated intervention for changing how you feel about certainty and tolerance of greater uncertainty. So, let's begin with a demonstration based on an experience of Shauna's. She had always wanted to visit England but had never traveled overseas. She felt overwhelmed by all the uncertainties, which put her in a state of doubt and indecision.

EXERCISE EXAMPLE: Shauna's Indecision About London

Shauna started by rating her current level of certainty about making the trip. Because there were so many unknowns, she decided that she felt only 20% certain about the trip. She knew how to book a flight and trusted the airline to honor the ticket once she'd paid, and she knew what to pack for the trip. Beyond that, though, there were so many uncertainties for her to think about.

Next, she considered all the questions she'd need to answer before she could make a decision. She'd need to know about hotel accommodations, the travel itinerary, financing the trip, safety and security issues, health coverage, currency exchange, and the like. Given the breadth of the unknowns, she decided she'd need to feel 80% certain before deciding to book the trip, which is reflected in the following figure.

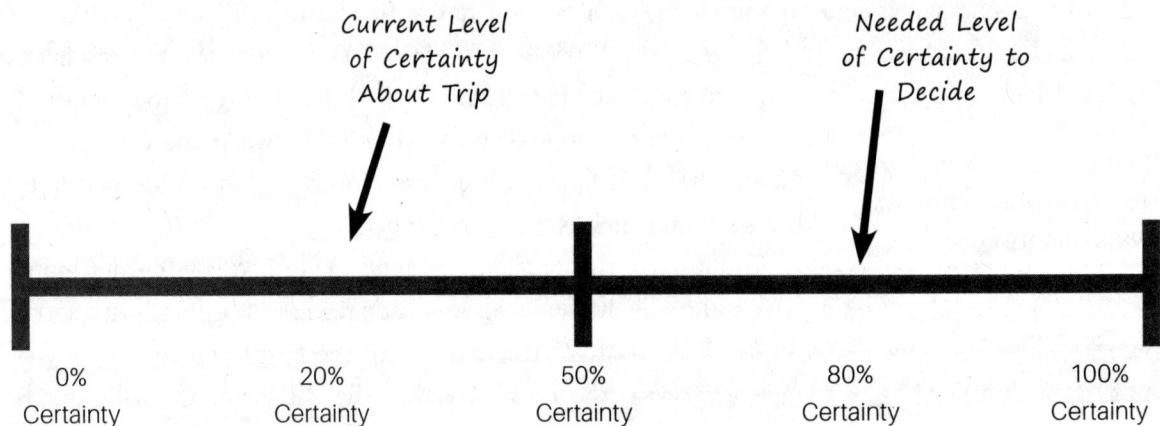

| 0% Certainty | 20% Certainty | 50% Certainty | 80% Certainty | 100% Certainty |

The final step in this exercise is the most important. Shauna made a list of what she could do to raise her feeling of certainty from 20% to 80%. She listed things like securing accommodations at a familiar hotel chain, arranging transportation from the airport to the hotel, obtaining additional travel health insurance, and so on. After that she asked herself three questions:

- Have my efforts to raise my feeling of certainty from 20% to 80% been successful? Have they eased my doubts and gotten me closer to a decision?

- Do I really need to feel 80% certain? Are there other tasks and activities I do in daily life with less than 80% certainty?

- Is the effort to raise my feeling of certainty worth the effort?

Shauna completed the exercise, but she was overcome with a sense of futility. It was clear to her that all her efforts to raise her feeling of certainty had failed. So, what was the alternative for her? Accept that planning an overseas trip is filled with uncertainties. With this in mind, Shauna planned and did her best to be well prepared, and she decided she'd go even if she couldn't achieve a comfortable level of uncertainty.

Now that you've considered Shauna's experience, try using this intervention to tackle one of your troublesome doubts.

EXERCISE: Certainty Gradient

In the space below, write about an excessive doubt you're experiencing related to a past action, belief, or impending decision. Remember, the doubt is distressing because it's associated with a fear of the unknown.

_____

_____

Next, using the gradient depicted below, identify the current level of your feeling of certainty associated with the doubt expressed as a percentage. After this, consider the level of certainty you would need to feel to banish all doubt associated with this past action, belief, or decision. Again, mark this as a percentage of your feeling of certainty associated with the doubt. On a separate sheet of paper, list all the information, reassurance, actions, and the like you'd need to raise your feeling of certainty to the desired level. Then complete the following certainty gradient, as Shauna did.

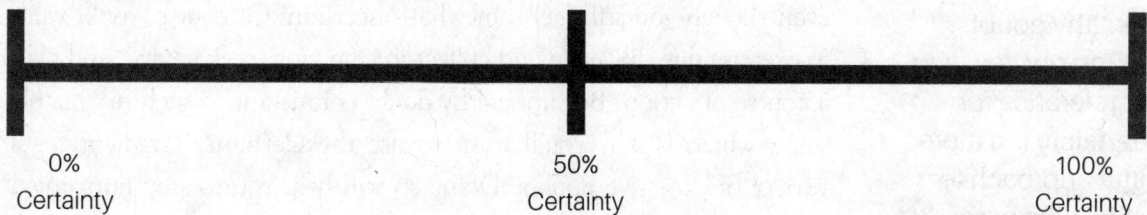

|—————————————+—————————————|

0%
Certainty

50%
Certainty

100%
Certainty

Once you've completed the certainty gradient, answer the following questions.

Have my efforts to raise my feeling of certainty been successful? Have they eased my doubts and gotten me closer to a decision or resolution?

_____

_____

Do I really need to feel _____% certain? Are there other tasks and activities I do in daily life with less than _____% certainty?

_____

_____

Is the effort to raise my feeling of certainty worth the effort?

_____

_____

Were you able to raise your feeling of certainty from a low level to the higher, desired level by gathering more information or obtaining reassurance about the future? Do you really need to have such a high feeling of certainty in order to let go of the past, reaffirm a belief, or make a decision? Overall, do you think all this effort was worth it?

If this intervention left you feeling frustrated, that all of this work seems quite futile, then you've done it correctly. The purpose of the Certainty Gradient is for you to experience how difficult it is to raise your feeling of certainty. Even if you can raise your certainty feeling by 10% or 20%, it typically won't be enough to ease your excessive doubt. The only reasonable alternative is to raise your tolerance for uncertainty—that is, make a decision or reaffirm a belief even though you still feel somewhat uncertain. Of course, you'll want to exercise due diligence and collect information, seek advice, and plan a course of action. But unhealthy doubt is resistant to such reasonable steps, which is why you'll want to use the Certainty Gradient for a variety of excessive doubts. Doing so will help you to stop pursuing a stronger feeling of certainty. Know, though, that your efforts to change

> Striving for a greater feeling of certainty is not the answer for unhealthy doubt. Working on elevating your tolerance for uncertainty is a more fruitful approach to dealing with excessive doubt.

how you think about certainty will not be enough. You also need to take action and practice embracing novelty, or the unexpected.

The Novelty Challenge

When are you most likely to experience an intolerable feeling of uncertainty? Chances are that unfamiliar, ambiguous, and unexpected situations are especially difficult because they are associated with a lot of unknowns. If you have low tolerance for uncertainty, a novel situation will trigger a surge of doubt that can leave you bewildered or even paralyzed. Think back to the last time you started a new job, the first dates with your current partner, the birth of your first child, or a medical treatment for a newly diagnosed condition. In all of these first-time experiences, you likely faced many uncertainties that intensified self-doubt. You likely had so many questions: *How will it turn out? What if I can't handle the situation? What harm or dangers are in store for me? What if I fail?* These questions capture the sense of uncertainty that often characterizes that which is novel. So, it's understandable why you might try to avoid or escape anything that is novel when you have low tolerance for uncertainty.

> Novel situations provide a unique opportunity to confront your fear of uncertainty and the crippling sense of doubt that accompanies it.

When did you last think *My life is too boring and routine. I need to do something new, something outside my comfort zone?* If you don't like uncertainty, this thought would be quite foreign to you. But getting outside your comfort zone, exposing yourself to the novel and unpredictable, is one of the most potent interventions for increasing your tolerance of uncertainty. Putting together a list of novel, unfamiliar experiences that you could experience several times a week is a great start. Shauna wrote the following.

Sign up for Pilates.	Initiate a casual conversation with coworker twice a day.
Invite a friend for dinner.	Take a weekend trip to a new city.
Go to the movies alone.	Shop for a new car.
Make a comment at the department meeting.	Politely disagree with a friend's opinion.
Change my hairstyle.	Join a book club sponsored by a local library.

Shauna found all the listed experiences uncomfortable to varying degrees because they have a lot of unknowns and so elicited a considerable fear of uncertainty. As Shauna reviewed the list, she was filled with doubt that she could actually follow through. Of course, some of the experiences she listed would be much harder for her than others, but each would provide her with an opportunity to confront her fear of the unknown. Shauna found that once she did some of the things multiple times, her discomfort decreased. This signaled that her intolerance of uncertainty was also on the decline. An unintended consequence of all this work on novelty was that Shauna felt more independent, resilient, and confident in herself. Her self-doubt was diminished, and she felt ready to tackle the even more difficult experiences.

The following exercise will allow you to change your tolerance of uncertainty through exposure to the novel.

EXERCISE: The Novelty Experiences Worksheet

In the worksheet below, list up to ten tasks, activities, or situations that are novel, unfamiliar, unpredictable, or ambiguous for you. Choose experiences that you can integrate into your daily routine and that you can repeat over and over. The experiences should span the range from slightly difficult to very difficult. In the second column, rate the expected difficulty of each experience from 0 (would have no difficulty doing this activity) to 10 (would have maximum difficulty doing this activity). Beginning with the least difficult experiences, start doing them, and place a checkmark in the last column to record each time you do. Gradually work your way up to the most difficult novel experiences in your list.

Novelty Experiences	Expected Difficulty Level (0–10)	Number of Times Practiced
1.		
2.		
3.		
4.		
5.		
6.		
7.		
8.		
9.		
10.		

Did you find that the more you practiced a novel experience, the easier it got? Were you able to progress from the easier experiences to the most difficult? If you succeeded in working through all the experiences in your list, you can always challenge yourself with more difficult novelty experiences. The more you do, the better you'll get at tolerating uncertainty and practicing a healthier form of doubt.

If you find you're disappointed in this intervention, you may have chosen experiences that were too easy or too difficult. Be sure to include several experiences in the moderate difficulty range. Also, you need to practice over and over again. One or two exposures to any experience will not be enough to reduce your discomfort. If you're patient, this intervention for intolerance of uncertainty is particularly potent because it's an action-oriented approach to doubt.

Distress Management

Whether in response to your fear of uncertainty or more general difficult and threatening situations, changing how you think and act requires determination and effort. The interventions for uncertainty in this chapter will cause you distress. This is unfortunate because it is the distress associated with uncertainty that makes it so intolerable (Freeston et al. 2020). So, as you work on becoming more tolerant of uncertainty, you'll need to use strategies to deal with distress. Many of these are well-known CBT interventions used to treat anxiety. The following is a brief review of several management strategies that are particularly well suited for uncertainty distress.

> **Repetition:** The most effective intervention for anxiety is repeated, practiced exposure to a perceived threat or danger. The same is true for any distress that is felt because of an intolerance for uncertainty. If you repeatedly confront your uncertainty, the feeling of anxiety, distress, or discomfort caused by the uncertainty will be reduced. It will take time and involve many repetitions, but the distress will eventually subside. It's impossible to say how long it'll take, and the decline in distress will be uneven, but if you stick with it, the distress will weaken. (For step-by-step instruction on exposure, see *The Anxiety and Worry Workbook* by Clark and Beck, 2023.)

> **Know your unknowns:** If you find uncertainty distressing, it's likely there is a possible outcome that is particularly unwelcome. Consider Shauna's doubts about planning her trip to London. It involved many uncertainties, but the one that bothered her most was the possibility of having a medical emergency while overseas. Once she pinpointed her most feared outcome, she got to work gathering information about how to deal with a medical emergency in England. She also had the interventions from chapter 6 to help her correct her possibility error. Developing a contingency plan for dealing with a medical emergency and learning to treat her feared outcome as possible but not probable helped

Shauna reduce her distress. You can use the same tactics once you know the ultimate unknowable that's driving your uncertainty.

Go with the flow: It's natural to do whatever you can to eliminate distress. But often the effort to find relief can prolong distress, even when it's effective in the short term. Acceptance and mindfulness are effective interventions for managing distress (see Forsyth and Eifert 2016 for further discussion). Essentially, these interventions involve allowing your emotions to ebb and flow naturally without effort to control or manipulate them. For intolerance of uncertainty, you acknowledge your distress about not knowing an outcome and then allow the feeling to simply be there, knowing that you've done all that can be done to prepare yourself for what lies ahead. After much planning and preparation for her London trip, Shauna came to realize that 70% certainty was all she could achieve. She would have to accept the remaining 30% uncertainty and let the associated distress take its natural course without judgment or effort on her part.

Wrap-Up

The desire for certainty is at the heart of excessive doubt. As you saw in this chapter, low tolerance for uncertainty makes you more susceptible to excessive doubt, whereas high tolerance can inoculate you against unhealthy doubt. How you think about uncertainty and the need to know determines your tolerance level.

In this chapter I presented several cognitive behavioral interventions that can help you adopt a healthy attitude toward uncertainty. If you're a low-tolerance person experiencing frequent and unrelenting doubt, practicing these interventions can transform how you think about uncertainty and the need to know. You can learn to think like a high-tolerance individual. But it will take time and patience. Your natural inclination will be to search for answers that will tell you what to expect. Learning to sit with the uncertainty, to accept it as an unavoidable aspect of living, will require conscious, effortful correction using this chapter's interventions. As a way of determining your progress with this chapter, retake the Measure of Uncertainty Tolerance presented in chapter 1 and compare your scores. Do you see any improvement in your tolerance for uncertainty?

Doubting the doubt and strengthening your tolerance for uncertainty are core strategies for overcoming disabling doubt. In the last chapter, we'll take what you've learned and apply it to the problem of indecision, one of the most important and pervasive aspects of doubt that has a profound impact on your quality of life.

CHAPTER 11

Become More Decisive

Do you struggle with indecisiveness (see chapter 2)? Did you score high on the Measure of Indecisiveness? If so, it's likely that you overthink issues and search for more information than is necessary to confirm you're making the right decision. Indecision is made worse by holding counterproductive decision-making beliefs that contribute to your hesitancy to take decisive action. And what about your decision-making strategies? Do you procrastinate until it's too late or make ill-informed, hasty decisions to get through the stress of decision making as quickly as possible?

As you'll see from the interventions in this chapter, the key to being more decisive is to reverse the processes that are responsible for indecisiveness. You'll learn how to know when you've done enough research or information gathering to make a decision, and which beliefs promote efficient decision making. Decision making is an active process, so I'll highlight decision-making strategies that offer a critical-thinking approach to the problems and challenges of daily living.

> Healthy decision making is so important to mental health that it is often a major goal in psychological treatments for depression, anxiety, and other emotional conditions.

But first, consider Nina's dilemma involving several major life decisions.

Nina's Story: *No Easy Answer*

Nina was nearing the fortieth anniversary of her employment. Several similarly aged coworkers had retired, but Nina continued to work, mainly for financial reasons. However, the work was starting to wear on her. And it seemed like management, too, was hinting that retirement might be the best option. But Nina was torn and unable to decide on the right course of action. She was into her second year of indecision, and the stress and worry were taking a toll on her mental health. Nina's health was another area of indecision for her. She had been experiencing stiffness and pain in her joints but couldn't decide whether to see a doctor or just chalk it up to aging.

Nina had strained relations with family. She had not spoken to her oldest son in years, and she'd last seen her grandchildren when they were born. *Should I try to reconnect with my son*, she wondered, *or wait for him to make the first move?* Her husband had been dead for five years, and since his passing she'd avoided her in-laws. She didn't know if she should take action to reconnect or just forget about them. Nina knew she needed to make other lifestyle changes, such as reach out to old friends, join some organized activities, and be more active. But she couldn't decide what she wanted, so she did nothing.

Nina was paralyzed by indecision, and she could feel herself slipping further into depression. For Nina, tackling her indecisiveness was going to be critical to reversing the downward spiral into depression.

Knowing When Enough Is Enough

Decisive people are quicker to make decisions and require less information than indecisive individuals. Let's say you're at a pricey restaurant deciding what to order. Do you take a long time to read over every item on the menu? Do you ask the waitstaff about the ingredients used in several dishes? Do you ask the person you're with for their opinion and then total the cost of the meal in your head? Or do you scan the menu, see a dish that sounds delicious, and promptly order it? The former individual is indecisive, requiring an unusual amount of information to arrive at a decision (much to the annoyance of their dinner guest, not to mention the waitstaff). The second person is decisive and requires much less information to make a quick decision.

> Adopting a structured approach to decision making is a necessary step in breaking the cycle of indecisiveness.

Breaking indecisive dithering requires effort and intention. You cannot follow your natural inclination and use the decision-making process that is most comfortable. Instead, you will need to follow strict rules, a decision-making protocol that encourages greater efficiency. The following decision-making process is designed to streamline information gathering and to emphasize everything that is needed to make an efficient and informed decision.

EXERCISE: The Decision-Making Protocol

Start by selecting an issue that requires a decision. Choose a high-valued decision that is causing you considerable distress and unrelenting doubt. Then answer the six questions that focus on key aspects of decision making. The protocol concludes with you describing specific steps you must take to arrive at a decision. An example from Nina is provided.

Describe the decision you need to make:

Should I retire? I could easily stay for another five years at least, but I'm finding the work more tiring. Also, management is dropping hints that it's time to go.

1. What is the decision outcome that you would most regret?

    I retire and then can't make it financially. I'm forced to take a service-related job with low pay and terrible hours. It would be so humiliating to be in that situation.

2. What information do you already have to make a decision?

    a. *I know I can stay on; I have a good union job, seniority, and job security.*

    b. *I know how much I've saved. I'm eligible for Social Security and own my house.*

    c. *I met with my financial advisor, who did some calculations and says I have enough to see me through until I'm ninety-two years old.*

    d. *My doctor thinks I have too much stress in my life, that I need to take more time for me; it would help with the depression.*

3. How can you ensure that you won't have an outcome that you'll regret?

    I honestly can't think of what more I can do to ensure greater financial security than to continue working. I can't know the future, what the economy will be like, how long I'll live, or what my health will be like.

4. What's a reasonable time limit for making the decision?

    I'll give myself another three months and then decide whether to stay at work for another five years or retire.

5. List the possible consequences of delayed decision making.

   a. Prolonged stress, anxiety, and worry caused by fretting about what to do.

   b. Making a decision seems to get harder and harder the longer I dither; I feel a sense of paralysis, that I can't move on with my life.

   c. The indecision makes me feel weak and helpless; it's probably contributing to my depression.

6. List what could be gained by deciding within your set time limit.

   a. I'll feel a sense of accomplishment.

   b. I'll have broken the paralysis and moved on with my life and faced the inevitable.

   c. There will be less stress and anxiety, because dithering over what to do is more stressful than making a decision and dealing with the outcome.

   d. I think my friends are getting tired hearing me talk about my indecision; they'll be relieved that I've put it behind me.

7. Describe a step-by-step action plan you'll follow to arrive at a decision.

   a. I'll ask the three coworkers my age who retired how they're doing.

   b. I'll make a list of questions and meet with my financial advisor one more time.

   c. I'll talk to my supervisor about staying on at work and try to get a sense of the direction the company is headed and whether she foresees any layoffs.

   d. I'll make an extensive list of pros and cons of not retiring, including how much better off I'll be financially by working another five years.

   e. I'll make a definitive decision based on the information at hand and not based on how I feel or on my fear of the unknown, which will exist whether I continue to work or retire.

Describe the decision you need to make:

_____

_____

1. What is a decision outcome that you would most regret?

   _____

   _____

2. What information do you already have to make a decision?

   a. _____

   b. _____

   c. _____

3. How can you ensure that you won't have an outcome you'll regret?

   _____

   _____

4. What's a reasonable time limit for making the decision?

   _____

   _____

5. List the possible consequences of delayed decision making.

   a. _____

   b. _____

   c. _____

6. List what could be gained by deciding within your set time limit.

   a. _____

   b. _____

   c. _____

7. Describe a step-by-step action plan you'll follow to arrive at a decision.

a. _____

b. _____

c. _____

d. _____

This protocol is a useful tool for breaking free of indecision based on intolerance for uncertainty, unrelenting doubt, and fear of the unknown. It's designed to help you make a reasoned decision rather than one driven by emotion. You can use the protocol repeatedly to work through a variety of decisions. It's a process you can master with practice. But don't hesitate to ask for help. A therapist, trusted friend, or family member might have different insights that you'd find helpful. Sometimes it's hard to make decisions rationally because of dysfunctional beliefs, which you may need to deal with before you can use the protocol effectively.

Confront Dysfunctional Beliefs

Our beliefs about the decision-making process influence how we make important decisions in life. Unhealthy decision-making beliefs will make it difficult to use The Decision-Making Protocol. Nina, for example, would have difficulty implementing a more efficient decision-making strategy for retirement if she believed *there was only one correct option*. This would trap her in an endless cycle of searching for the one and only correct choice. On the other hand, if she believed that *most decisions have more than one good option*, she'd be more decisive because she wouldn't waste time trying to discover the one true choice.

Are you aware of decision-making beliefs that contribute to your indecisiveness? Maybe you've tried to be more decisive, but your best efforts have been thwarted by an unhealthy belief system. The next exercise gives you an opportunity to determine the health of your decision-making beliefs.

EXERCISE: Range of Decision-Making Beliefs

The twelve exaggerated decision-making beliefs from the Decision-Making Belief Scale in chapter 2 are listed on the left below. To the right of each belief is an alternative version that might be more helpful in making decisions. Place an X on the line to indicate whether you're more inclined to agree with the indecisive or the decisive belief. Make sure to base your rating on what you actually believe rather than on what you think you should believe.

Indecisive Belief		Decisive Belief
1. Most decisions are permanent; they can't be changed later.		Most decisions can be changed or modified later if necessary.
2. A quick decision is more likely to result in a poor outcome.		Taking time to decide does not always guarantee a better outcome.
3. For every decision, there's only one correct option.		Decisions often have more than one good option.
4. It's important to feel certain that you've made the right decision.		Feeling certain isn't a criterion for determining that I made the right decision.
5. The more time you take to make a decision, the less likely you are to make a choice you later regret.		It is always possible that I'll regret a choice regardless of how long I take to decide.
6. Never settle for second best when making a decision.		Sometimes it's better to compromise, to lower your expectations.
7. You should always have a good feeling about your decisions.		A decision can be right even if it doesn't feel right at the time.
8. It's always better to postpone a decision than risk making a less satisfactory decision.		Sometimes the cost of postponing a decision is greater than the cost of a less satisfactory decision.
9. You should always wait until you have no doubts before deciding what to do.		There is always some doubt when making a decision.

Indecisive Belief		Decisive Belief
10. Decisions should be as risk free as possible.		Minimizing risk is only one factor to consider when making a decision.
11. A missed opportunity is more tolerable than a disappointing decision.		The cost of a missed opportunity due to indecision can be greater than the cost of a less desirable decision.
12. You should always seek the opinion of others before making a decision.		Seeking advice from others when deciding is wise, but excessive reassurance seeking can interfere in decision making.

Realistic expectations about the decision-making process are critical to being more decisive.

Were more of your *X*'s toward the left side of the line or on the right? If most were to the right, then you have a pretty healthy view of decision making. You might need to look elsewhere for the seeds of your indecision. But if you had several *X*'s to the left, you might want to consider correcting these beliefs. They are likely undermining your efforts to be a more efficient decision maker. Use the next worksheet to begin the process of correcting unhelpful decision-making beliefs.

EXERCISE: Belief Correction Worksheet

The following questions guide you through the process of using your personal experience to evaluate the accuracy of a decision-making belief. Make copies of the worksheet so you can use it on a variety of unhelpful beliefs. It and other worksheets are available for download at this book's website, http://www.newharbinger.com/55756.

State the unhelpful decision-making belief:

_____

_____

_____

What personal experiences support the accuracy or truthfulness of this belief?

1. _____

2. _____

3. _____

4. _____

What personal experiences cause you to question the accuracy or truthfulness of this belief?

1. _____

2. _____

3. _____

4. _____

What can you conclude about the belief based on what you've written? Does the evidence against the belief outweigh the evidence in support of the belief? If so, consider changing the belief so it encourages more efficient decision making. Write the corrected belief in the space below.

My corrected decision-making belief:

_____

_____

_____

Once you arrive at a corrected decision-making belief, it's important to put it into practice. Every time you face a significant decision, remind yourself of the unhealthy belief, why the belief is inaccurate, and of the greater accuracy of the corrected belief. You can then engage in decision-making strategies that are consistent with the corrected belief.

> You need to correct dysfunctional beliefs about decisions before you can implement an effective decision-making plan.

Critical-Thinking Skills

Decision making is the most common trigger for doubt. And when we're faced with a decision, the doubt we experience can be helpful or harmful. As noted in the book's introduction, doubt is helpful in decision making when it contributes to critical thinking. Excessive or harmful doubt will cause avoidance, procrastination, and even paralysis when you're trying to decide the best option. Mastering the art of critical thinking is another way of ensuring that your doubt is helpful.

Critical thinking is a deliberate, goal-directed approach to making decisions and solving problems. When people think critically they skillfully use reason, observation, and evidence-based information to improve the chance of achieving a desired outcome (Halpern 1998; Young 2023). The critical thinker also engages in self-correction by questioning their assumptions, becoming aware of their thinking errors and biases, and evaluating multiple perspectives. Because of this, critical thinkers make better decisions than individuals with fewer critical-thinking skills.

> Break through indecision and procrastination by engaging in the critical-thinking process. It begins with acquiring accurate and reliable information that leads to a well-reasoned and informed decision.

Critical thinking is both an attitude and a set of thinking skills. Critical thinkers are thoughtful, open-minded, and flexible. They are highly motivated and willing to exert considerable mental effort to tackle problems using mental skills that are planned and based on evidence. They are able to correct errors in their reasoning and exhibit a willingness to abandon unproductive strategies (Halpern 1998). When stuck in unproductive doubt, they know when to bring the full force of critical thinking to decision making.

Considerable research has gone into identifying the core cognitive skills that define critical thinking. Although perspectives differ, the following six critical-thinking skills are most relevant for effective decision making.

Problem clarification and information gathering: Be clear and specific about which problem, issue, or concern will be addressed by the decision; gather a reasonable amount of relevant information.

Analyze and evaluate the information: Separate evidence-based information from asserted claims or opinions; break down complex information into smaller, manageable parts; determine the reliability of your sources; discard irrelevant information.

Generate possible choices: Based on reliable and accurate information, list several, often competing, possible choices; these should be logical conclusions drawn from the available information.

Evaluate the choices: State clear and specific outcomes associated with each choice; list the pros and cons associated with each outcome; determine the likelihood that a choice will result in your desired goal or outcome.

Be aware of and self-correct thinking errors and biases: Recognize biases in your thinking such as all-or-nothing thinking, overgeneralization, jumping to conclusions, having an overly positive or negative filter, magnifying or minimizing effects, and the like; identify faulty beliefs and inconsistent judgments.

Choose, implement, and review: Make a decision and then write a step-by-step plan for implementing it; after a short period of time, evaluate the outcome of your decision; make any adjustments to the plan that improve the chance of you reaching your desired goal.

Critical Thinking in Decision Making: An Illustrative Example

To illustrate how critical thinking can improve your decision-making efficiency, imagine you're facing one of the most important, emotionally painful decisions in your life. For months you have been paralyzed by indecision on whether to stay with or leave your intimate partner. You are strongly committed to the relationship. In the early years, you were in love. The relationship was loving, supportive, and affirming and had moments of fun, excitement, and romance. But all of that has changed. You've grown apart and you no longer feel loved or respected. Your needs and interests are brushed aside, and you've had intense arguments that are never resolved. Insults have replaced tenderness, and you fear the relationship is becoming toxic. You've threatened to leave but your partner seems not to care. For months, you've been paralyzed by indecision: *Should I leave or should I stay and try to work it out?*

When faced with such a monumental, heart-wrenching decision with life-changing consequences, it's easy to see how you might feel paralyzed by indecision. You might continue in a relationship that is threatening your mental health, or you might make an impulsive decision driven by the emotional intensity of the moment. Either way, you might end with a poor decision. Let's take a look at how critical thinking might help you break through indecision and lead to a better outcome.

1. **Clarify and inform:** The problem is you've become depressed, discouraged, and trapped in a loveless relationship, and some of your partner's behavior borders on emotional abuse. You spend three months gathering information on causes of intimate relationship conflict, the treatment for and response to it, marital separation, depression, and living alone and without love. You consult online resources and printed material and speak to friends who've gone through a similar experience. You decide to meet with a marriage and family counselor to seek further insight and guidance.

2. **Analyze and evaluate:** You divide the information into two categories: evidence for staying versus evidence for leaving. You consider whether the information is personal experience and opinion or based on expert advice and research. During your evaluation,

you discard information that is irrelevant for your decision to leave or stay. You may come across other sources that deserve further investigation and follow up.

3. **Generate possible choices:** Based on your research you decide there are three possible choices: (1) it's better for you to leave the relationship as soon as feasible, (2) it's better to stay and work on creating your own happiness, or (3) it's best to renew your commitment to the relationship as long as it's contingent on meaningful and lasting change.

4. **Choice evaluation:** You determine the immediate and long-term consequences for each choice and your personal well-being. You list the advantages and disadvantages of each choice. In terms of disadvantages, for example, regret might be a greater possibility with the first choice, further decline in your mental health with the second, and increased anger and resentment with the third choice if meaningful change doesn't materialize.

5. **Identify and correct thinking biases:** As you think about what's best, you realize you have certain biases and faulty beliefs that could cloud your judgment. Perhaps you were raised to believe that divorce must be avoided at all costs and is a sign of failure, and you assumed that no divorced person could ever be happy. Perhaps you were raised to believe that it is primarily a woman's responsibility to make a (heterosexual) relationship work. Perhaps you had a negative experience with counseling in the past. Perhaps you find it hard to go against the advice of your older sister, who is conversative and highly opinionated. You actively challenge these biases as you decide the best choice for you.

6. **Choose and take action:** You decide the third option is best for you. You'll stay for another six to twelve months and seek meaningful change in the relationship. You'll start by having a heart-to-heart conversation with your partner. You'll talk about your unhappiness and what is not working for you in the relationship. You'll ask that they engage in relationship counseling. If they do not agree, you'll leave. If they do agree to counseling, you'll have an opportunity to define meaningful change. It may be that with the help of a therapist, you'll decide to end the relationship. You can then shift your focus to creating a new life as a single person.

Do you see how the critical-thinking process can help you overcome indecision, avoidance, and procrastination when you're facing even the most difficult decisions in life? Living through an intimate relationship breakup is a heart-wrenching experience with long-term implications. It can be a traumatic loss that leaves lasting emotional scars. But living with indecision can be equally harmful. Critical thinking can help you break through this conundrum by giving you the tools to take charge of your life. The next worksheet gives you an opportunity to apply the critical-thinking approach to an important decision you've been dreading.

EXERCISE: The Critical-Thinking Worksheet

Select an important issue that requires a decision and answer the following questions, which are designed to guide you through the critical-thinking process. Most of the questions require an extensive answer, so you'll need to use extra paper (the worksheet is also available for download at http://www.newharbinger. com/55756). This is not an exercise you can do quickly. It will be most effective if you spend time thinking deeply about your responses to each question.

What is the focus of your indecision? Be specific about the problem you are facing.

_____

_____

List the relevant information you've sought for the problem you're trying to resolve. (Use additional paper if necessary.)

1. _____
2. _____
3. _____
4. _____

Explain the reliability, accuracy, and relevance of each piece of information. Assess the truthfulness of the information as it relates to your indecision.

_____

_____

_____

_____

_____

_____

List the possible choices based on your evaluation of the information.

1. _____
2. _____
3. _____

State the pros and cons of each choice as it relates to you. How do you anticipate each choice will impact your life and well-being?

1. _____
2. _____
3. _____

List the errors and biases in your thinking. How can each be corrected?

_____

_____

_____

_____

State the choice you've selected. Describe a step-by-step action plan you'll follow to implement the choice.

_____

_____

_____

_____

_____

_____

Did the critical-thinking process help you overcome your indecision? Again, there can be no absolute guarantee of the outcome of any decision, but indecision is rarely the best option. You have a better chance of achieving your goals if you use critical thinking when making decisions. But merely writing down a decision will have little impact on your quality of life. You need to back up the critical-thinking process with action to take control back from indecision and create a better life for yourself.

Wrap-Up

If you've experienced indecision related to an important issue, you know the dithering process can have a paralyzing effect on your ability to function. Being in a state of indecision can be highly stressful, and it increases the likelihood that opportunities for improving your quality of life and well-being will be missed. But indecisiveness can be beaten. In this chapter, three interventions were presented that can make you a more effective and efficient decision maker. And if you are better at making decisions, you will be overcoming a harmful form of doubt.

Concluding Remarks

We all doubt. Not only is doubt an unavoidable state of mind, it is necessary for our very survival. But doubt can turn on us and become a serious impediment to our health and well-being. Excessive doubt can cause a paralysis of indecision that traps you in a state of helplessness, despair, and diminished quality of life. But it doesn't have to be this way. As you've learned in this workbook, you can transform unhealthy and self-defeating forms of doubt into assets that help you solve the problems and challenges of everyday living.

The first step to gaining control over doubt begins with understanding the complexity of this mental state. In the first six chapters you learned how intolerance of uncertainty, indecisiveness, needing to know, perfectionism, and risk aversion can turn any doubt into an unrelenting form of mental anguish. The exercises in these chapters gave you opportunities to identify what causes your periods of runaway doubt.

The second part of the workbook highlighted three types of doubt: obsessive, relationship, and religious. I was highly selective in my focus for this book and know that I excluded other types of doubt you might be familiar with, such as self-doubt, interpersonal doubt, and sexual orientation doubt. In fact, we are capable of doubting just about every experience. But obsessive, relationship, and religious doubts are among the most common and deleterious forms of excessive doubt, which is why I chose them. Doubts in each of these domains are inevitable, but the assessment tools in these chapters helped you determine whether your doubts are harmful or helpful.

The final chapters provided step-by-step instructions and worksheets for using three intervention strategies to counter unhealthy doubt: challenging the doubt, increasing your tolerance of uncertainty, and learning to act decisively. These are not simple strategies, because doubt itself is not simple. It requires determination, effort, and practice to master the skills required to break the bonds of excessive doubt. Having come this far with the workbook, you've acknowledged a problem with doubt, have a desire to make meaningful change, and have the intervention tools needed to make this change. It is my hope that you've found in this workbook insights to inspire you anew to work on curbing the excesses of your doubts. May all your doubts lead to a better path forward.

Acknowledgments

For decades I've offered cognitive behavioral therapy to a host of people struggling with obsessive compulsive disorder (OCD). Doubt has been a central feature of their struggle. Most people with OCD know their doubts are excessive, unreasonable, and debilitating, and yet they feel powerless in their presence. I was curious that this form of pathological doubt seemed impervious to rational argument and so began a long journey into researching and writing about OCD and its various processes, including doubt.

This workbook is a culmination of my ideas on excessive doubt and indecision borne out of clinical experience and research. But organizing this work into a coherent and comprehensible form of written communication is a team effort. I am thankful for the many individuals who played an important role in its production. I appreciate their wise advice and expert opinions. I am grateful to the senior management of New Harbinger who gave me another opportunity to publish with them. Ryan Buresh, acquisition editor, has been an undying support in seeing this project through to completion. As always, working with Ryan was a most rewarding experience. His thoughtfulness, understanding, and gentle persuasion were of great encouragement throughout the arduous writing process. I am also indebted to Vicraj Gill, New Harbinger senior editor, for her insight, sensitivity, and clarity of thought that contributed greatly to the book's structure, organization, and comprehensibility. James Lainsbury, copy editor, waged a tireless and meticulous campaign for improved legibility for which I am grateful. The great cover design was inspired by Amy Shoup. I am especially grateful to Dr. Robert Leahy for the insights and clinical wisdom he has offered in the foreword. As a renowned author and much cited expert on cognitive behavior therapy, Dr. Leahy's illuminating observations on doubt are a highly valued contribution to this workbook.

Special mention goes to Bob Diforio, my literary agent, who has been integral to this publication and so many others. Bob has an unrivaled expertise of the publishing world, and I am so grateful to be the recipient of his unique wisdom and unwavering support. Last, to my family, Nancy, Natascha, and Christina: I appreciate the years of their listening to my doubts, and their patience and understanding as I talk about my work and efforts to set my ideas down with pen and paper.

References

Antony, M. M., and R. P. Swinson. 2009. *When Perfect Isn't Enough: Strategies for Coping with Perfectionism*. 2nd ed. Oakland, CA: New Harbinger Publications.

Buhr, K., and M. J. Dugas. 2002. "The Intolerance of Uncertainty Scale: Psychometric Properties of the English Version." *Behaviour Research and Therapy* 40: 931–45.

Carleton, R. N. 2016. "Into the Unknown: A Review and Synthesis of Contemporary Models Involving Uncertainty." *Journal of Anxiety Disorders* 39: 30–43.

Carleton, R. N., P. J. Norton, and G. J. G. Asmundson. 2007. "Fearing the Unknown: A Short Version of the Intolerance of Uncertainty Scale." *Journal of Anxiety Disorders* 21: 105–17.

Chiang, B., and C. Purdon. 2023. "A Study of Doubt in Obsessive-Compulsive Disorder." *Journal of Behavior Therapy and Experimental Psychiatry* 80: 101753.

Clark, D. A. 2024. *This Is What Anxiety Looks Like: Relatable Stories, Targeted Solutions, and CBT Skills for Lasting Relief*. Oakland, CA: New Harbinger Publications.

Clark, D. A. 2019. *Cognitive-Behavioral Therapy for OCD and Its Subtypes*. 2nd ed. New York: Guilford Press.

Clark, D. A., and A. T. Beck. 2023. *The Anxiety and Worry Workbook: The Cognitive Behavioral Solution*. 2nd ed. New York: Guilford Press.

Clark, D. A., and A. T. Beck. 2010. *Cognitive Therapy of Anxiety Disorders: Science and Practice*. New York: Guilford Press.

Crawley, R. A. 2010. "Closure of Autobiographical Memories: The Effects of Written Recounting from First- or Third-Person Visual Perspective." *Memory* 18: 900–917.

Czyżowska D., E. Gurba, N. Czyżowska, and A. M. Kalus. 2020. "Intimate Relationship and Its Significance for Eudaimonic Well-Being in Young Adults." *Health Psychology Report* 8: 155–66.

Curran, T., and A. P. Hill. 2019. "Perfectionism Is Increasing Over Time: A Meta-Analysis of Birth Cohort Differences From 1989 to 2016." *Psychological Bulletin* 145: 410–29.

Egan, S. J., T. D. Wade, R. Shafran, and M. M. Antony. 2014. *Cognitive-Behavioral Treatment of Perfectionism*. New York: Guilford Press.

Forsyth, J. P., and G. H. Eifert. 2016. *The Mindfulness and Acceptance Workbook for Anxiety: A Guide to Breaking Free from Anxiety, Phobias, and Worry Using Acceptance and Commitment Therapy.* 2nd ed. Oakland, CA: New Harbinger Publications.

Freeston, M. H., J. Rhéaume, H. Letarte, M. J. Dugas, and R. Ladouceur. 1994. "Why Do People Worry?" *Personality and Individual Differences* 17: 791–802.

Freeston, M., A. Tiplady, L. Mawn, G. Bottesi, and S. Thwaites. 2020. "Towards a Model of Uncertainty Distress in the Context of Coronavirus (COVID-19)." *Cognitive Behaviour Therapist* 13: 1–15.

Gaudreau, P. 2019. "On the Distinction Between Personal Standards Perfectionism and Excellencism: A Theory Elaboration and Research Agenda." *Perspectives on Psychological Science* 14: 197–215.

Gaudreau, P., B. J. I. Schellenberg, A. Gareau, K. Kljajic, and S. Manoni-Millar. 2022. "Because Excellencism Is More Than Good Enough: On the Need to Distinguish the Pursuit of Excellence from the Pursuit of Perfection." *Journal of Personality and Social Psychology* 122: 1117–45.

Germeijs, V., and P. De Boeck. 2002. "A Measurement Scale for Indecisiveness and Its Relationship to Career Indecision and Other Types of Indecision." *European Journal of Psychological Assessment* 18: 113–22.

Graham, J., B. A. Nosek, J. Haidt, R. Iyer, S. Koleva, and P. H. Ditto. 2011. "Mapping the Moral Domain." *Journal of Personality and Social Psychology* 101: 366–85.

Halpern, D. F. 1998. "Teaching Critical Thinking for Transfer Across Domains: Dispositions, Skills, Structure Training, and Metacognitive Monitoring." *American Psychologist* 53, 449–55.

Knowles, K. A., and B. O. Olatunji. 2023. "Intolerance of Uncertainty as a Cognitive Vulnerability for Obsessive-Compulsive Disorder: A Qualitative Review." *Clinical Psychology: Science and Practice* 30: 317–30.

Lazarov, A., R. Dar, N. Liberman, and Y. Oded. 2012. "Obsessive-Compulsive Tendencies and Undermined Confidence Are Related to Reliance on Proxies for Internal States in a False Feedback Paradigm." *Journal of Behavior Therapy and Experimental Psychiatry* 43: 556–64.

Lee, D. 2013. "Decision Making: From Neuroscience to Psychiatry." *Neuron* 78: 233–48.

Lunn, J., D. Greene, T. Callaghan, and S. J. Egan. 2023. "Associations Between Perfectionism and Symptoms of Anxiety, Obsessive-Compulsive Disorder and Depression in Young People: A Meta-Analysis." *Cognitive Behaviour Therapy* 52: 460–87.

New International Version. 1995. *The NIV Study Bible.* 10th anniversary ed. Grand Rapids, MI: The Zondervan Corporation.

O'Connor, K., and F. Aardema. 2012. *Clinician's Handbook for Obsessive Compulsive Disorder: Inference-Based Therapy.* Chichester, UK: Wiley-Blackwell.

O'Connor, K., F. Aardema, and M.-C. Pélissier. 2005. *Beyond Reasonable Doubt: Reasoning Processes in Obsessive-Compulsive Disorder and Related Disorders.* Chichester, UK: Wiley.

Peretz, C. 2005. "Faith and Doubt." American Jewish University. December 17. https://www.aju.edu/ziegler-school-rabbinic-studies/our-torah/back-issues/faith-and-doubt.

Rachman, S., A. S. Radomsky, and R. Shafran. 2008. "Safety Behaviour: A Reconsideration." *Behaviour Research and Therapy* 46: 163–73.

Rajaee, S. 2022. *Relationship OCD: A CBT-Based Guide to Move Beyond Obsessive Doubt, Anxiety, and Fear of Commitment in Romantic Relationships.* Oakland, CA: New Harbinger Publications.

Rassin, E., P. Muris, I. Franken, M. Smit, and M. Wong. 2007. "Measuring General Indecisiveness." *Journal of Psychopathology and Behavioral Assessment* 29: 60–67.

Robichaud, M., and K. Buhr. 2018. *The Worry Workbook: CBT Skills to Overcome Worry and Anxiety by Facing the Fear of Uncertainty.* Oakland, CA: New Harbinger Publications.

Salkovskis, P. M. 1991. "The Importance of Behaviour in the Maintenance of Anxiety and Panic: A Cognitive Account." *Behavioural and Cognitive Psychotherapy* 19: 6–19.

Seif, M. N., and S. M. Winston. 2019. *Needing to Know for Sure: A CBT-Based Guide to Overcoming Compulsive Checking and Reassurance Seeking.* Oakland, CA: New Harbinger Publications.

Shafran, R., S. J. Egan, and T. D. Wade. 2023. "Coming of Age: A Reflection of the First 21 Years of Cognitive Behaviour Therapy for Perfectionism." *Behaviour Research and Therapy* 161: 104258.

Shafran, R., S. Egan, and T. Wade. 2018. *Overcoming Perfectionism: A Self-Help Guide Using Scientifically Supported Cognitive Behavioural Techniques.* 2nd ed. London: Robinson.

Stoeber, J., and K. Otto. 2006. "Positive Conceptions of Perfectionism: Approaches, Evidence, Challenges." *Personality and Social Psychology Review* 10: 295–319.

Summerfeldt, L. J. 2004. "Understanding and Treating Incompleteness in Obsessive-Compulsive Disorder." *Journal of Clinical Psychology* 60: 1155–68.

Upenieks, L. 2021. "Changes in Religious Doubt and Physical and Mental Health in Emerging Adulthood." *Journal for the Scientific Study of Religion* 60: 332–61.

Wooden, C. 2016. "Pope Francis: Everyone Experiences Doubts in Their Faith Life." *America: The Jesuit Review.* November 23. https://www.americamagazine.org/faith/2016/11/23/pope-francis-everyone-experiences-doubts-their-faith-life/.

Young, R. 2023. "The Power of Critical Thinking: Enhancing Decision-Making and Problem-Solving." Forbes Coaches Council. July 28. https://www.forbes.com/councils/forbescoachescouncil/2023/07/28/enhancing-decision-making-and-problem-solving/.

David A. Clark, PhD, is a clinical psychologist, and professor emeritus at the University of New Brunswick in Canada. He is author of several books on depression and anxiety, including *Overcoming Obsessive Thoughts*, *The Anxiety and Worry Workbook*, *The Anxious Thoughts Workbook*, *The Negative Thoughts Workbook*, and his most recent publication, *This Is What Anxiety Looks Like*. He has coauthored several books with the pioneer of cognitive behavioral therapy (CBT), Aaron T. Beck, including *Cognitive Therapy for Anxiety Disorders*.

Foreword writer **Robert L. Leahy, PhD**, is author or editor of several books, including *If Only...: Finding Freedom from Regret*, *The Worry Cure*, and *The Jealousy Cure*. He is director of the American Institute for Cognitive Therapy in New York, NY, and clinical professor of psychology at Weill Cornell Medical College.

MORE BOOKS from
NEW HARBINGER PUBLICATIONS

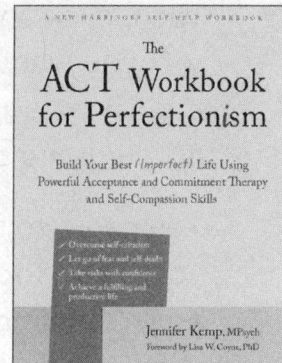

Did you know there are **free tools** you can download for this book?

Free tools are things like **worksheets**, **guided meditation exercises**, and **more** that will help you get the most out of your book.

You can download free tools for this book—whether you bought or borrowed it, in any format, from any source—from the New Harbinger website. All you need is a NewHarbinger.com account. Just use the URL provided in this book to view the free tools that are available for it. Then, click on the "download" button for the free tool you want, and follow the prompts that appear to log in to your NewHarbinger.com account and download the material.

You can also save the free tools for this book to your **Free Tools Library** so you can access them again anytime, just by logging in to your account! Just look for this button on the book's free tools page. ➤

+ Save this to my free tools library

If you need help accessing or downloading free tools, visit **newharbinger.com/faq** or contact us at **customerservice@newharbinger.com**.